# The Knowledge Channel

# The Knowledge Channel

## Corporate Strategies for the Internet

*by*

*Langdon Morris*

toExcel

*San Jose   New York   Lincoln   Shanghai*

# The Knowledge Channel

Published by toExcel

For information address:
toExcel
165 West 95th Street, Suite B-N
New York, NY 10025
www.toexcel.com

ISBN: 1-58348-287-3

Library of Congress Catalog Card Number: 99-62872

Printed in the United States of America

# Table of Contents

# List of Figures

# *1* *Introduction*

## Purpose of this report

Based on new technologies that have become vital new media for human communication, the electronic marketplace has developed from an interesting possibility into an important reality during the last decade. While telephone and cable television companies spent millions of dollars on the initial development phases of the as-yet unsuccessful interactive television systems, the internet emerged as a powerful social phenomenon.

Built upon a powerful and flexible technological foundation that utilizes the existing global telecommunications infrastructure and the rapidly spreading personal computer, the internet promises to become the basis of a significant global mass market. As yet, however, neither the full social character of the internet nor its ultimate commercial potential are clear, as mature business models have not emerged.

Nevertheless, the interaction between the internet's social and commercial aspects is one of its most compelling characteristics, for the internet has already shown that it can support new kinds of communities, virtual communities. This social phenomenon suggests the possibility of not only a new market, but a new kind of market.

How the internet will develop in the coming decades is an intriguing question, and with the exponential growth of internet use, millions of dollars of venture capital backing dozens of internet-related companies, and high IPO valuations, there is suddenly a lot at stake.

## The organizing model

We humans have what seems to be both an insatiable need and a persistent desire to communicate with one another, and it is into this context that the domain of electronic commerce is significant. In a sense, therefore, what we are exploring here is simply the application of information technology to the phenomenon of human communication.

But of course the more deeply one looks, the more one finds that it is not so simple. The need of humans to communicate is also a significant factor in human commerce, and therefore the full gamut of individual and social motivations and consequences come into play. It is precisely the combination of these forces, as expressed through the intricacies and complexities of this emergent marketplace, that offers such intriguing possibilities for both entrepreneurs and investors.

The birth of electronic commerce as a new marketplace is occurring as the result of more than a century of economic and technological development. The shift from the industrial age to the knowledge age is the large historical backdrop for this process. More recently, the development of digital technology and the convergence of many forms of analog communication onto a set of digital standards is the primary means and the driver of change: Information technology and related services now compose approximately one-sixth of the U.S. economy. It is the development of digital technology, then, that has led to the emergence of a new interactive marketplace of electronic commerce (which will in turn lead to further evolution of the economy). (figure 1)

Reflecting this model, the evolution of the economy is described in Chapter 2, followed by a discussion of the new interactive market in Chapter 3. For those not familiar with the technical issues, a brief discussion is presented in the Appendix.

In Chapter 4 we turn our attention to the issues of corporate strategy which emerge as a consequence of these changes, and finally in Chapter 5 we examine the view towards the future, both short and long term.

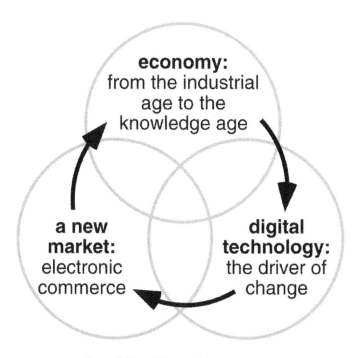

(figure 1) Organizing model & report contents

## Summary of key points

Among the many ideas that we explore in this report, the seven points summarized below are the keys to understanding the emerging character of the new marketplace and the role that corporate strategy must play in positioning your firm to face the new threats and opportunities that the internet brings:

1   Paradigm change

The use of the internet at the leading edge of electronic dialog and electronic commerce will not be a short-lived phenomenon, but rather one that will endure as a significant factor in social and commercial life for many decades. One of the primary reasons for this is that the internet is the only mass medium yet to emerge that is fully coherent with the shift from the industrial economy to the knowledge age.

## 2    Critical mass

The growth of the internet since the invention of the World Wide Web in 1990 has been a sustained exponential process. In 1995, it was estimated that 10 million people used the internet. During 1996, this number grew to 20 million, and in 1997 it is estimated at 50 million. If current growth rates continue, by the year 2000 there will be between 300 and 400 million users. The positive feedback of network effects – that more people are drawn to participate as more people are participating – suggests that the actual numbers could very well be even higher, particularly if new, high-speed means of access such as cable modems become common.

## 3    The internet rupture

The evolution of the information industry from the 1970s through the 1990s is a story of dramatic growth. The rapid emergence of the internet during this decade has led, suddenly, to a rupture that is causing dislocations throughout the business world. Companies find their existing strategies imperiled, while at the same time the internet offers an abundance of new opportunities that must be considered.

## 4    The knowledge channel

As we observe a widespread shift from supply-driven markets to demand-driven markets, the individual comes to the fore as a learner and a consumer with increasing power in the marketplace. The internet is perhaps the ideal tool for communication with this new kind of customer through the "knowledge channel," the direct linkage for the sharing of critical knowledge directly between producers and their customers, and among customers, in internet-based communities.

## 5    Internet communities

The internet is changing the dynamics of global society by enabling groups of like-minded individuals to form themselves into communities regardless of where they live. As communities share interests that may be related to companies and products, many of them will have significant commercial impact.

## 6    From differentiation to commodity

During the last twenty years, technology has been a force of change throughout the business world. To their surprise, many premium producers suddenly found themselves competing in commodity markets when innovative newcomers used technology to strip away their differentiated advantage. The internet will be a catalyst of the same dynamic as the wide dispersion of knowledge will strip away the protection that many once-differentiated products and distribution channels formerly enjoyed.

7    Technology and strategy

Consequently, it is vital to take a strategic view of the internet, and to use it as a strategic tool to help position your company for the coming waves of competition. Business models must be carefully crafted to reflect the new structures and niches that electronic commerce is beginning to offer.

• • •

As new technologies extend the reach of economic activity into new domains, it is clear that while the internet shares important characteristics with the broader economy of which it is a part, it is also unique in many ways, important ways, that are the focus of our inquiry here.

# $2$ *The New Economy*

## The knowledge age

Scanning the broad history of economic development we see the evolution of the global economy from agricultural roots in pre-industrial societies, through 200 years of industrialism and up to the present. Our era has variously been called the Information Age, the Knowledge Age, the Age of Creation, and the Age of Communication, and the fact that there is not widespread agreement about the proper name is revealing, for it indicates that there is not yet a clear understanding of the forces that are compelling us forward.

Among the defining characteristics of our era, certainly the preeminence of computer technology and the consequent explosion of data must be at the forefront.

In and of themselves, however, data are of very limited value. When we filter them we can obtain information which is more useful, and if we process information correctly we may be able to get knowledge, which is more valuable still.

This suggests that we can define a value chain with data at the beginning, followed by information, and then knowledge. Understanding would be next, progressing finally to wisdom at the end. This model has been suggested by management professor, cybernetician, and author Russell Ackoff.[1]

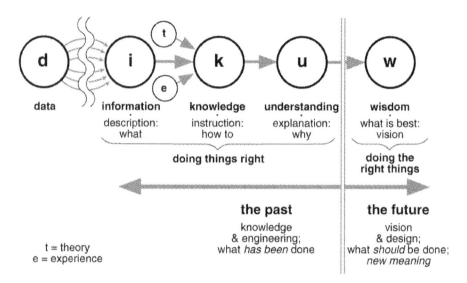

(figure 2) Russell Ackoff's path to wisdom

The model shows that information merely provides a description, the "what," whereas knowledge contains instruction in the "how." Understanding is concerned with "why," and wisdom is the perspective towards the future in terms of vision and "what is best."

Each transition, from data to information; from information to knowledge; from knowledge to understanding; and from understanding to wisdom, requires work, but in each case the work takes a different form.

The step from information to knowledge comes about through the integration of three distinct elements. First there is the information itself, encoded as a description in writing or in any medium. The second requirement is theory, which provides context through which information may be interpreted. The final component is experience, the pot in which the stew of information and theory are cooked to produce knowledge.

This process of integration is literally how new knowledge is created. It is also called "learning," and it can be accomplished only by individuals, for it is an activity of the conscious mind.

When individuals join together to form organizations, the learning process of many can accumulate into knowledge that confers advantage in the marketplace. Hence, managers at leading companies such as Hewlett Packard, Sony, Toyota, and GE, are adept at identifying the critical performance factors in their markets, and then delivering superior value to their customers. They have mastered the learning process.

Since the creation of new knowledge through learning is the driving force in today's economy, we believe that our society is making the transition from industrialism to the knowledge age.

This emergence is evident in subtle and interesting ways. For example, the pattern of investment among Japanese manufacturing companies during the 1980s reveals a steady shift away from investments in hard assets and a consistent increase in research and development (R&D) investments. These, in fact, are investments in learning.[2]

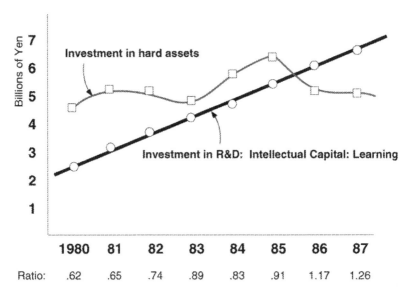

(figure 3) Ratio of investments in R&D and
hard assets by all Japanese manufacturing companies, 1980—1987

This is compelling evidence that the Japanese grasped the shift to the knowledge age more than fifteen years ago, an interesting awareness in the context of global competition.

The development of the knowledge age and the overwhelming importance of the learning process at the core of this new economy has many other implications as well. First and foremost, it is clear that since the learning process is an activity of the individual, it is the individual who now moves to the center of economic life. The industrial model of supply-driven mass consumerism is no longer sustainable, and must undergo significant reformulation for the knowledge age.

In the consumer marketplace, this means that companies reorganize themselves to address demand-driven markets of individuals rather than large demographic groups.[3] The infrastructure to support this shift emerged in a preliminary way with the introduction of the personal computer, and now continues to develop through the connection of the personal computer to the internet, which brings each individual into a global dialog.

In this new environment, individuals stand alone as markets of one, but ironically now many products no longer stand alone, because they are networked via the internet to deliver interactive, client-server based communications, applications, and services.

Another change is that the influence of mass media has made consumers more knowledgeable, and their preferences and expectations evolve much more quickly than in the past. In many markets it is simply no longer realistic to introduce a consumer product and expect it to last very long.

Finally, there has been a subtle shift from a focus on government and defense-related research and development to a focus on consumer markets at the leading edge of commerce, a process called "trickle-up." Trickle up markets are predominating because fighting for a share of the mass market drives a learning process that totally concentrated and contains the maximum possible feedback.[4]

As a result of these forces, products and services that once had life spans measured in years are now revised, upgraded, or replaced in months, weeks, or in the case of web pages, even days.

Whereas mass production enabled manufacturers to focus on progressively lowering their costs, today's trickle-up competition shifts the focus to time, compressing the viable duration of all products in the marketplace.

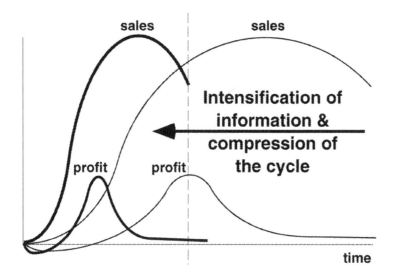

(figure 4) Compression of the product life cycle[5]

Continual advances in technology also cause rapid obsolescence for all products that incorporate information technology (which soon will be nearly all of them).

Among the responses to these pressures are dramatic changes in manufacturing processes (emphasizing flexibility and product platform thinking); increasing emphasis on learning and design (to provide more enduring value); and the creation of new services (with sustainable margins).

Over the years, the computer industry has evolved along such a progression, moving from "dumb terminals" to PCs with greater value-added at each step in the technology chain, while product life spans of sub-components and systems have shortened with each generation.

Today, companies such as Hewlett Packard achieve very fast cycles for new product development. In the home computer market, for example, HP engineers design a new product every three to four months to keep up with the evolving marketplace.

The same shift occurred in the auto industry, where it used to require up to seven years to design a new car, while today companies including Chrysler, Toyota, and Ford have compressed this to as few as 30 months by reconceiving the infrastructure and the work processes that support the creation of new knowledge. Individuals and teams work very effectively in the linked tasks of learning and design that characterize the learning-based process of creating new technology.

Thus, even in the auto industry, the quintessence of the industrial age, we see the emergence of knowledge as the critical differentiating factor.

## The shift to values

Increasing competition and compression of the sales cycle are also driven by the trend towards globalization. Rapid economic growth during the 1970s and 1980s prompted companies throughout the world to increase their production capacities, with the result that today's capacity exceeds sustained demand, further intensifying competition in the marketplace.[6]

During the 1970s, a new emphasis on product quality was exemplified by Japanese auto and electronics manufacturers, which captured significant shares of global markets because they achieved higher quality standards than their American and European competitors. As a result, customers began to experience, and then to expect, higher quality.

Soon, however, the focus on quality was not sufficient to differentiate a company or a product. Many sought, therefore, to differentiate themselves by offering new services.

In the mid-1980s the emphasis shifted again, this time to improving the quality of the services and to designing the kinds of experiences that customers have. Simply offering a service was no longer sufficient.

At each step, a new set of implicit standards emerged that quickly became widely expected. Further, the new standards did not simply replace the old ones, they were added. Thus, manufacturers saw that they had to strive for continuous increases in product quality, and at the same time to offer new services which had also to be progressively improved in quality.

This progression in the source of added value is enabled by an increasing flow of information between the company and its customers, a key factor that is now emerging as an important source of differentiation.

A leader in this area is Saturn, the company that GM established to rethink everything about the car business. Saturn shifted the emphasis away from the car itself, putting it instead on the relationship between the company and the customer, and on the process of buying a car.

In the Saturn model, the car itself is almost an afterthought. What matters most is the customer's experience of the dealership, the sales person, and even the service representative. The underlying rationale is clearly that when you make and sell a product for people whom you respect and care for, you naturally do it in a manner that enables you and your customers feel good about the whole transaction. Hence, you offer a top quality product at a fair price, and you make the buying experience pleasant. Further, the initial transaction is followed by continuing high levels of service.

As simple as this sounds, it is certainly not a description of the process of buying a car in America in the 1990s or at any time in the past, except perhaps for the era of the Model T. By following this model rigorously, Saturn has rapidly become the most highly regarded American car company. And to ensure that predatory sales practices do not creep into the corporate culture or the customer's experience, Saturn does not hire sales people who have already sold cars elsewhere, as it proved to be too difficult for them to abandon their win-lose habits.

In the end, the commitment to doing business this way becomes an expression of human values, where differentiation comes from the "soft" aspects of human affairs rather than from advanced technology. This is the logical next step in the evolution of the economy, and it will be a key factor in the development and maturing of the internet.

## *Values*
↗
## The *experience* of the customer
↗
## Services
↗
## Products

(figure 5) The shift towards values

Many business leaders have grasped this shift toward values, and they have integrated this principle into both management and public relations.

New organizations such as The Natural Step and Business for Social Responsibility research and promote business practices that are socially and environmentally sustainable, and they are attracting membership from the entire economic spectrum, including small businesses, Fortune 500 companies, and advocacy groups.

At the same time, corporate philanthropy has become a major source of social capital both in the U.S. and throughout the world. Companies such as Target stores, a division of Dayton Hudson, donate a fixed percentage of their profits to charities in the communities in which they do business. As a part of its marketing effort, Target then promotes its donations policy on signs throughout their stores, and even on shopping bags and cash register receipts.

Other companies, such as Working Assets, a credit card and long distance phone reseller, are in business with the explicit purpose of generating profits that can be channeled into social causes. In 1996, Working Assets donated more than $2.5 million to 36 charities that were selected by its customers.

The reemergence of values as a critical differentiating factor in the marketplace is an expression of the growing awareness that we may have drifted too far from our responsibilities as members of local communities and a global society. Hence, leaders search for ways to bring human values into all aspects of commerce even as they now explore the internet as a new medium through which commerce can be conducted.

The development of the knowledge economy is evidence of the continuing movement towards understanding and wisdom as fundamental aspects of our culture, but it would be an exaggeration to suggest that we have become a culture of understanding or wisdom. The overwhelming prevalence of human suffering among the billions of poor, the pervasive cultural malaise among the rich, and environmental destruction all over the planet makes it clear that we have a long way to go.

Nevertheless, as the knowledge economy emerges from the industrial age that preceded it, we are engaged in a transition that has decisive implications for entrepreneurs and investors who must assess where future opportunities lie.

It is clear in this context that electronic commerce is fully coherent with the underlying dynamics of the knowledge age, and may indeed make important contributions to its full development.

# 3 The New Interactive Marketplace

## A new mass medium

The mass media of newspapers, magazines, radio, television, and movies have been important influences in modern society throughout the 20th century. Our very ideas, images and experiences of modern life are intimately linked with the impact of these media on our thoughts and perceptions of reality.

Enveloped in this intimacy, we sometimes forget that these media are not universal realities, but simply cultural and historical artifacts of our own creation. After all, a medium is simply something that is "in the middle," and these mass media are in the middle of the communications loop between people. Thus, they provide "mediated communications," communications that are not conducted face to face, but through other means.

The powerful impact of media is not limited to our culture or our times. The art works and tools of all humans convey messages across centuries and millennia, and they still communicate with us today whether they are prehistoric cave paintings, stone tools, carved bones, or contemporary radio and television broadcasts.

In the recent history of human civilization, the invention of printing as a medium of mass communications extended the reach of the written word, and profoundly impacted human culture. Martin Luther, for example, intended to boldly provoke debate among his fellow clergy, but his 95 theses found their way onto a recently invented printing press and rapidly spread throughout all levels of German society. He found himself, to his surprise and dismay, at the forefront of an historical movement instead of the theological debate he envisioned.[7] Hence, the invention of moveable-type printing transformed the one-to-one medium of writing into the first one-to-many medium of mass communication.

## Writing
One to one
The Bible

## Printing
One to many
The 95 theses of Martin Luther

## Telegraph
One to one

## Telephone
One to one

## Radio
One to many
Churchill; DeGaulle; Hitler; Roosevelt

## Television
One to many
Philippines; South Africa

## Fax
One to one
Intifada; Berlin Wall

## Internet
One to one; One to many; Many to many
Tiananmen Square; WWW; ?

(figure 6) The evolution of media

In the 19th century, the telegraph and telephone applied electricity to problem of human communication across great distances. The telephone is primarily a one-to-one communications medium, although a modest many-to-many capability emerged with the invention of the conference call.

The radio and its more addictive cousin the television are the defining one-to-many technologies of the 20th century. Their invention created the concept of "broadcasting" as we know it, and proved to be powerful forces for social change. During World War II, Churchill, de Gaulle, Hitler, and Roosevelt all used the radio to address their nations and inspire the war effort.

In our times, television plays a prominent role in shaping perceptions of the world during crisis, bringing world events into our homes on nightly news broadcasts or CNN's coverage of the crisis du jour.

The influence of television is even more insidious in the mundane world of day to day life simply because of how it conveys images of living. McLuhan pointed out that the real message of television is not the news it brings, but in the very experience of watching television itself, and the continuing confusion between the medium and its messages is also one of the defining characteristics of modernity.[8] In the end, the method of television is seduction, and the enduring message is simply to continue watching.

Now with the spread of the internet and its offspring the World Wide Web, society has a new medium of mass communications. For the first time there is the possibility of a more complex form of mass communication because the internet is uniquely a medium for simultaneous and non-simultaneous "many-to-many" communications.

This many-to-many capability is one of the most important reasons for the growth of the internet and its rapid assimilation into society. New kinds of communities that take advantage of this capability are emerging, "virtual communities" that are held together by shared interests which transcend distances and political boundaries.[9] And since the number of internet users appears to be approaching critical mass, it seems that this new medium may also become a significant new marketplace.

Morgan Stanley estimated in 1995 that the number of personal computers in use was about 150 million, and growing at nearly 40% per year. This would put the number of PCs in use in the year 2000 at between 300 and 400 million. The same study suggested that 10 million people used the internet in 1995, and forecast a doubling of use from year to year thereafter.[10] Statistics from 1996 and 1997 suggest that this forecast is on track, or possibly a bit too conservative. At these growth rates, by the year 2000 nearly all PC users will also be on the internet, (as well as many devices that operate autonomously).

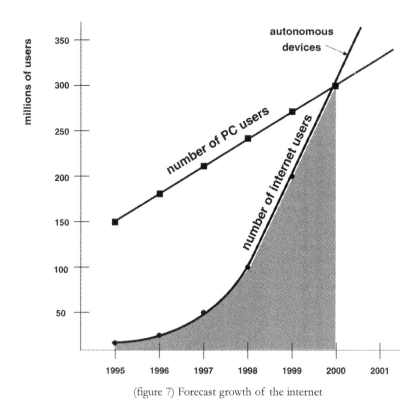

(figure 7) Forecast growth of the internet

With numbers of this magnitude, entrepreneurs and investors are drawn to explore the possibilities that the internet may offer, and to develop new technologies that will bring the internet more deeply into everyday life for the hundreds of millions of people who may soon be active participants in this market.

## The information business

Among the many consumer electronic devices introduced during recent decades, the compact disc player, the fax machine, the VCR, and the personal computer have caused notable ruptures. Mike Shatzkin has pointed out that these products are successful because they enable people to do the same things that were done with earlier devices, but now more easily.[11] The compact disc displaces the cassette and the record; the fax machine displaces the post office and the telephone; the VCR augments or replaces broadcast television; and the PC displaces the typewriter, the post office, handwriting, the calculator…

The internet is now bringing about such a rupture, significantly influencing the direction of society and of commerce. As we will see, the evolution of the internet and its spread into the mainstream of global culture has the potential to displace broadcast media and their associated advertising paradigms. It may also displace existing fee-for-service business, some publishing, and a significant amount of retail shopping.

To gain an historical perspective on the emergence of the internet and its relation with the broader information marketplace, it is helpful to examine the development of the broad sector of industries that compose what has been called "the information business."

This concept was developed in 1979 by the Harvard University Program on Information Resources Policy. The program leaders developed a map that helped many to understand how different businesses and industry segments were part of a new information industry phenomenon of tremendous power and importance. The map also provided an early image of the shift to a new economy of information and knowledge.[12]

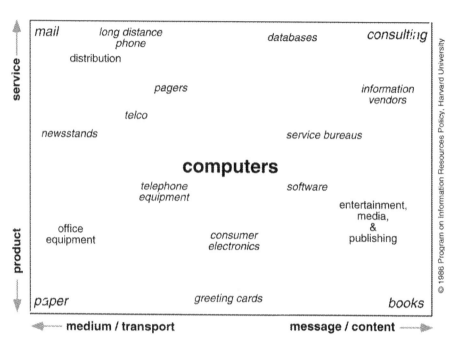

(figure 8) The information business map

The map is organized as a field, with the continuum from products to services on the vertical axis, and the continuum from transport and media to message and content on the horizontal. In this media space, then, industries and technologies are plotted, and clear relationships emerge.

The map shows, for example, that before electricity and digital technology were invented, the entire information business consisted of just the periphery.

While costs at the periphery are subject to the constraints of material commodities and therefore tend to rise, costs in the center, led by advances in the computer industry, have steadily declined in the fifty years of computing as performance has improved exponentially. In the last decade alone, there has been a 100-fold improvement in computer speeds even as prices have come tumbling down.

In fact, the map makes explicit an idea that many managers had experienced only intuitively, namely that the favorable economics in the center compels them to move that way to survive.

Hence, the program was supported by nearly 100 corporations and government agencies, most of which were positioning themselves to exploit the markets at the center of the map. Many of them, including AT&T, IBM, Apple Computer, used the map as a model to help them forecast the development of the information business through the end of the century, and to develop strategies that would help them capitalize on the underlying trends.

Most recognized that as computer technology became more powerful it would become ubiquitous, and distinct market segments would converge to create new kinds of products and services. Through the efforts of these companies and countless others, this indeed is happening much as it was predicted to happen.

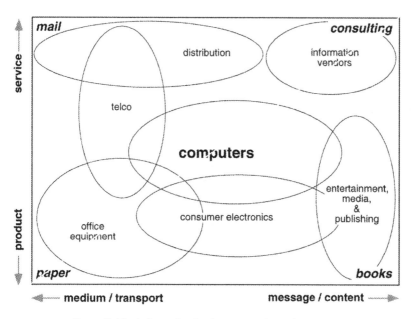

(figure 9) The information business map, circa 1985: Convergence

By the late 1980s this trend resulted in a technical convergence of many different applications of information technology towards a set of digital standards, which created the serious possibility of a universal "information appliance" at the center of the map. Telephones, televisions, and computers began to incorporate elements of each other, and it was clear to many industry participants that the full merger of these three fundamental technologies was only a matter of time. A more detailed discussion of this convergence is presented in the Appendix.

One application of convergent digital technology was expected to be interactive television, which would take advantage of new technical capabilities to offer many forms of entertainment, products, and services into the home. Pursuing this possibility between 1986 and 1995, cable television and telephone companies spent millions of dollars to develop the technology, but to date they have not been able to deliver services that generate significant market interest at an acceptable price.

Nevertheless, the phenomenon of convergence represented — and still represents — both a tremendous opportunity and a tremendous threat to the companies in these sectors, and likewise has enormous implications for companies in industries as diverse as publishing, entertainment, and even transportation.

For at the same time that interactive television attempted but failed to create a new market, the U.S. government was in the process of opening use of the internet to the private sector.

This immediately led to a period of rapid growth in the use of the internet for email, and since internet-based email displaces the postal service, the result was a bubble in the top of the information business map.

For the first time, computer-like cost dynamics were found at the periphery of the map, which implied the possibility of profound change in the underlying dynamics of many industries.

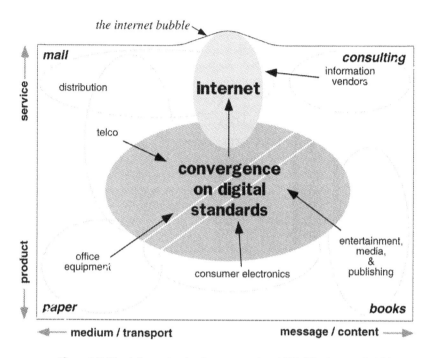

(figure 10) The information business map, circa 1995: The internet bubble

Accompanying the explosive growth of email was the invention of the World Wide Web in 1990 by Tim Berners-Lee, and the invention of the easy-to-use NCSA Mosaic browser by Marc Andreesen and colleagues in 1993. These two events caused an explosion of internet usage that has become, in effect, a rupture that has blown the top off the information business map.

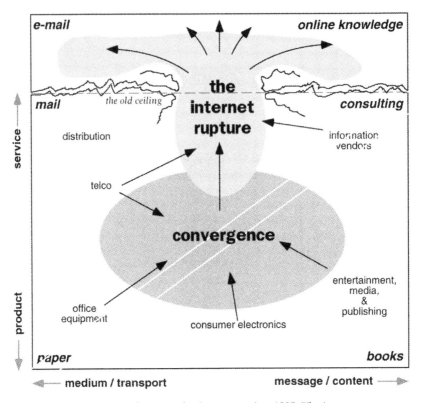

(figure 11) The information business map, circa 1997: The internet rupture

A key facet of the rupture is that by enabling companies to be in direct communication with millions of existing and potential customers, the internet has opened up a whole new territory on the map that is not subject to the same cost factors that applied at the top of the old map.

Thus, while the inherent cost characteristics of the postal service drives the price of postage stamps steadily upward even as service stagnates, the cost of email on the internet declines with the cost of computers, even as delivery occurs in minutes rather than days.

All across the top of the map, therefore, new forms of low-cost services enabled by the internet are suddenly juxtaposed with the higher cost services of the old paradigm, and innovative service providers are seizing opportunities to use the internet and exploit its favorable cost structure.

For example, book selling on the internet is one of the early commercial internet applications to show a (small) profit, and four powerful companies are now fighting for dominance in this market segment. Amazon.com, the pioneer, achieved more than $16 million in sales in its first two years, prompting retailers Barnes and Noble, Borders, and Crown (who between them operate thousands of retail book stores), to compete for a piece of the growing internet market.

## The technical infrastructure

All of this is happening because the basic technical characteristics of the internet are relatively simple, well adapted to the existing global communications infrastructure, and upwardly scalable.

Since the internet's underlying transmission network architecture uses the ubiquitous telephone system, it is very easy for individuals to get connected.

Four other factors also contribute to the likelihood of the internet's continued growth:

1.   TCP-IP: The technical standard by which internet messages are sent through the phone system, TCP-IP (Transmission Control Protocol – Internet Protocol) is independent of and easily adapted to nearly any kind of data type, including voice, music, text, graphics, photos, and video. Thus, any form of data can be sent over the internet.

2.   Open standards: As an open technology, any manufacturer can sell computer hardware and software products that work on the internet. No single manufacturer has control of the infrastructure technology, assuring widespread competition based on performance and price that creates continuing incentive for innovation.

3.   Platform independent: As an open system, the internet is platform independent for the local end user, so anyone can connect to the internet using almost any kind of network computer, personal computer, workstation, or mainframe terminal.

4.    Modem independent: The individual's connection to the internet is also speed independent, so individuals can connect their computers to the internet using any kind of modem from 300 baud to 10,000,000 baud.

Thus, it is the integration of the powerful technical infrastructure of the internet with the simple and elegant navigation paradigm of the world wide web browser that created the web and internet as we know it today.

As a result of these qualities, the internet is becoming a universal infrastructure that supports a tremendous variety of applications for many different kinds of users with widely diverging purposes.

When we compare this infrastructure with the capabilities of the proposed interactive television systems, it is apparent why demand for the internet has become so strong, while demand for interactive television remained weak.

The implementation model for interactive television was based on competing and very expensive proprietary transmission networks. Each provider would have total control over its network and the content that it provided.

In contrast, since the internet is a standardized and open transmission network, it is available to everyone who wants access, either as an information provider or as a recipient. Therefore, the real cost to operate the internet is relatively small to begin with, and since that cost is being spread over a pool of increasing millions of users, it is very inexpensive indeed.

Further, since all internet applications use the same technical infrastructure, the internet supports a vibrant and open discussion space and marketplace in which different ideas, products, and companies compete for attention based on the quality of their presentation and the terms that they offer. Anyone can connect to the internet at any time, for any purpose, and they do not require the permission of anyone else. The vitality and diversity that have emerged because of this openness is far richer and more interesting than any proprietary system could possibly achieve.

As a result of these factors, it is clear that the model underlying proprietary interactive television systems has already been displaced.

## The future of television

This does not mean, however, that television is finished. To the contrary, it is clear that the entertainment paradigm of television will remain as important as it has been for the last half-century.

It is the marriage of television with the internet that will be the next expression of digital convergence, as new forms of content and low-cost access for providers of products and services on the internet will merge with the mass markets and production standards of television.

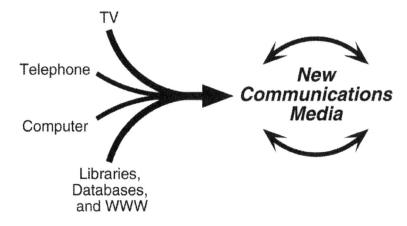

(figure 12) Convergence

Content is already migrating from television to the internet, as television broadcasters such as Fox, CNN, and NBC have created web sites to offer their television programming online.

Meanwhile, products such as WebTV, the Gateway Destination PC/TV, and the RCA-Compaq PC Theater pioneer the market for bringing internet content to the television. While their first generations are awkward and may not have much impact, continuing refinement of the technology and the interface design may lead to products that offer the best of both media. Microsoft's purchase of WebTV will provide critical capital and expertise to this process.

However, there is another important factor in the merger of these media. While the existing browser interface to the internet enables individuals to wander according to their interests by accessing web sites and "pulling" information from a web site onto their own computers, a new commercially-oriented phase of internet development has begun that is based on the concept of "push."

Push technology is part of the evolution of the internet into a fully developed broadcast medium that integrates key characteristics of television. What is pushed, of course, is a commercial message that accompanies programming content. It can come from anywhere on the internet directly onto your computer screen, just as a TV program is pushed from the broadcaster to your set via the airwaves, satellite, or cable.

While you choose the "channel" and a great deal of the content that is displayed on your screen, what you cannot choose is the accompanying advertising that pays for it all.

How successful and extensive internet push media will become depends on the willingness of customers to accept evolving formats, but with many millions of people susceptible to millions of advertising "impressions," there will be many attempts to develop the core technology and the applications.

The ultimate successes may emerge from hybrids that combine elements of push and pull to offer high degrees of customization, combined with advertising that is perceived as "tasteful," acceptable, or at least inoffensive.

Push media that integrate sophisticated search agents may enable providers to migrate towards the upper right corner of the information business map, creating differentiated value in products and services that precisely match complex needs.

New programming content will be developed that takes advantage of the strengths of the merged media, and at the same time the respective hardware platforms will gradually merge as the TV takes on functions of the PC, and vice versa. Soon there will be no difference between these devices, which will lead to an interesting structural competition between manufacturers in the two industries and the participants in their various distribution channels.

One key issue that will have to be resolved before the TV and the computer do merge is the problem of the viewing screen. While computer screens are mostly small and intended for individual use, television screens are large and easily viewed by groups and families. However, the quality of the images displayed on computer screens is better, particularly for text.

In the short term, NCI, the Oracle-Netscape affiliation, is among those developing software solutions for the integration of internet content with broadcast television.

Other solutions may lie in large flat-panel displays or projection displays, both of which are expected to become common in business settings. This increased volume will support price decreases, while the increasing quality of the images will soon make these devices suitable for home use for pure entertainment, reading text, and for browsing the web.

Over a period of the next decade or two, evolving concepts of home theater and new television standards such as HDTV will eliminate the issue entirely.

## The pivotal technical issue: Bandwidth

While the internet is already realizing much of the promise that was once expected of interactive television, some technical issues are still problematic.

In particular, user interfaces to the internet are still awkward, and there is a great need for improvement. The most significant problem, however, is the speed at which information, and particularly images, are viewed and downloaded.

The underlying factor here is infrastructure bandwidth. As noted above, an individual can connect to the internet at any speed, from 300 baud to 10,000,000 baud. The majority of current users are accessing the internet at speeds ranging from 2400 to 28,800 baud, but at speeds below 128,000 baud users must have a lot of patience.

Conversely, at speeds of 1,000,000 baud (1 megabit, or 1 million bits per second) and faster, the internet is easy to use and the depth and versatility of the information that can be easily accessed is impressive. Therefore, a critical factor in the spread of internet use will be how quickly a critical mass of users obtain access speeds of one megabit or faster.

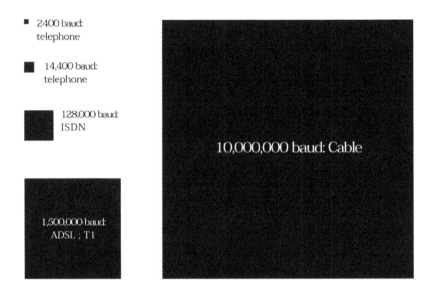

(figure 13) Bandwidth

This may happen quickly. During the last three decades, costs in the comput-er industry have fallen dramatically even as performance has increased. Likewise, the cost of communications bandwidth has also declined steadily. For example, in 1966, only 138 simultaneous conversations could take place between Europe and all of North America, and the price was high. Today, the North Atlantic telecommunications infrastructure supports approximately 1.5 million conversations, and at a much lower cost per connection.[13]

Some observers forecast that bandwidth performance will improve 1000-fold in the next ten years. If this happens, bandwidth will be essentially free, just as email is nearly free today. In this environment, the successful business models will be those that utilize prodigious amounts of bandwidth to deliv-er spectacular services, and those which use bandwidth to support distrib-uted computing. In contrast, compression technologies and bandwidth-fru-gal applications will be pushed aside.[14]

In the short term, cable and digital satellite modems operating at 4 to 10 mil-lion baud should soon be available. When these modems become common, internet use will explode beyond the early adopter stage and become firmly entrenched in the mainstream, assuring thereby the arrival of the new marketplace.

## A new kind of marketplace

As we have seen, the internet is a new medium through which more and more communications are conducted, and it is becoming not only a new marketplace, but with the power of many-to-many communications, a new kind of marketplace.

An aspect of the internet that is so intriguing is the breadth and depth of applications that it already supports. Any kind of digital content that can be sent using TCP-IP can use the internet as a delivery mechanism, and because TCP-IP is now an almost universal standard, the internet is being used for nearly every kind of communications.

Since widespread use of the internet is so recent, however, it is not yet clear which applications will ultimately become the most important, or the most successful commercially.

Further, developers and users have widely different purposes, so any definition of success will be multifaceted. Some, such as computer maker Dell and wine merchant Virtual Vineyards, seek commercial success, while others convey social, political, and advertising messages, and still others use the internet for aesthetic expression.

The fact that different kinds of purposes so readily coexist in one medium is notable in itself, and indicates how decentralization of access lends the internet medium such richness.

The cost of establishing a presence on the internet is so low for commercial applications that there is effectively no barrier to entry, particularly since the internet offers access to a huge and rapidly growing pool of potential customers. Going online provides immediate access to the global marketplace. Even better, internet users to date have tended to be better educated and wealthier than average, which makes them prime targets for electronic commerce.

The phenomenon of home shopping on television makes an interesting comparison. In the early days, the Home Shopping television network seemed to be an important market that offered great promise for the future. After a decade and many failed experiments, however, it is clear that home shopping on television is a small niche market that has much more to do with the social aspects of the transaction, and very little to do with the quality, value, or convenience that the medium might provide. Statistics indicate that many HSN and QVC customers are lonely, and that they buy because of the illusion of companionship. This cannot be an enduring or significant marketplace.

Today the combined revenues of HSN and QVC have stabilized at about $2.5 billion, while the revenue figures for broadcast and cable television advertising total approximately $36 billion.

It is too early to know what the ratio between retail sales and advertising revenues will be for the internet, but it is clear that online retail sales will far exceed those achieved through television shopping. Dell Computer alone is already selling more than $2 million worth of computers each day through the internet, or more than $500 million per year.

The implicit requirements for successful internet retailing are the same as with television — value means lower prices, and convenience means that people save time and have a broader selection. Amazon.com, for example, offers 2.5 million titles at discounts of up to 40%.

In contrast with the cable TV shopping channels, however, the growth opportunity for internet retail and all of internet commerce has more to do with the quality of the information and knowledge that can be made available through a wide variety of internet applications.

## Survey of internet applications

As the information business continues to grow and to drive radical change in global business, it is possible to see the outlines of an emerging new market structure. A recent report by The International Engineering Consortium suggests that three broad business categories will predominate in the coming decades: Information Content dealing with information and knowledge;

Information Transport dealing with the infrastructure and process of delivery; and Information Appliances, the tools used to create and disseminate content.[15]

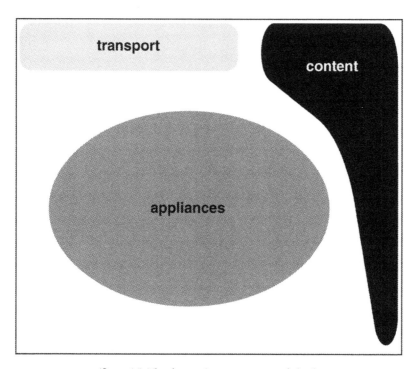

(figure 14) The three primary segments of the future

While it is clear that worthwhile and successful internet applications will be found in each of these three areas, our interest in this report is more focused. As our title implies, we are particularly interested in those content-related applications that are particularly knowledge oriented, as we believe that this is the area that will be most likely to support high value-added in products and services that command differentiated pricing.

By our count, there are seven knowledge-intensive types of content-driven applications for the internet, some of which also have important subsets. Note that most of the applications described below are necessarily pull oriented, but some can operate effectively in push scenarios, or in hybrid push and pull implementations.

1. Communications
   a. Email
   b. Virtual communities and interest groups
   c. Intranets
2. Retail commerce
   a. Shopping
   b. Fees for service
3. Business to business commerce
   a. The extranet
   b. Business information
4. Gambling and gaming
5. Programming content
   a. News
   b. Customized news
   c. Entertainment
   d. Education
6. Directories
   a. Of people and organizations (white & yellow pages)
   b. Maps
   c. Guides (restaurant, club, movie, etc.)
   d. Matching services
7. Marketing
   a. Branding and image management
   b. Personalized advertising

1.  Communications
    a.  Email
    b.  Virtual communities and interest groups
    c.  Intranets

a. Email. The internet began as a medium of communications for researchers in government and academia, and this core function is still one of its most vital uses. Now that people all over the world have access, the mundane business of sending email brings powerful competition to the post office and fax market. In 1996, for example, it is estimated that the U.S. Postal Service delivered 85 billion pieces of mail, while the internet delivered 95 billion email messages. From 1996 to 1997, America Online's email traffic grew from approximately 4 million email messages per day to about 16 million, or nearly 6 billion annually and still growing. Since it takes only about 1 minute to deliver a message from one AOL user to another, and about 15 minutes between an AOL user and a non-AOL user, the Post Office is clearly being marginalized in the junk mail delivery business.[16]

b. Virtual communities & interest groups. The internet is increasingly active as a medium that supports virtual communities. The capacity to engage in dialog with others who share specific interests has proven to be a compelling experience for the millions of people who are participating in these communities. Countless groups explore topics pertaining to all aspects of life, including religion, politics, culture, sports, food, entertainment, etc.

c. Intranets are a more focused form of the virtual community consisting of people who work within the same organization and who use the internet as a medium for internal communications to conduct their private business activities. This is one of the most rapidly growing applications of the internet since it enables organizations that are geographically distributed to communicate effectively at far lower cost than has previously been possible.

In addition, there are now sophisticated groupware tools that can be used to support shared information, structured dialog, the co-creation of knowledge products, and access to shared databases over the internet. This makes the internet into a useful management tool, particular for those who are responsible for (and frequently traveling to) geographically disbursed locations.

2.   Retail commerce
   a.  Shopping
   b.  Fees for service
   i.   Classified advertising
   ii.  Employment advertising
   iii. Dating services
   iv.  Access to databases and other information sources

a. Shopping. The current approach to internet retail commerce is awkward, and few retailers have been successful online. Given the character of face-to-face retail commerce, even the idea of online retail commerce is problematic.

Retailing in a store is an experiential process with strong tactile and interpersonal components, and these qualities are nearly impossible to replicate online. For example, a typical lipstick container is handled in the store eight times before it is bought, as each shopper examines the color to see if it is right.[17]

The internet cannot replicate this experience, which makes it unlikely that the internet can be used successfully for retail shopping where seeing and touching the product is critical.

Further, the process of making online transactions can be difficult and time consuming, which defeats one of the two advantages that distance retailing can offer, time savings.

Whereas clothing manufacturers need retailers to put their products on display in stores full of other brands of clothing in order to attract sufficient customers, products that do not require this form of browsing and which can be effectively sold without the intermediary of the retail store environment are the markets where the internet may offer an advantage.

This has been referred to as "transparent" commerce[18] because the distribution chain is vastly simplified and the customer comes into direct contact with a maker who is also the seller.

Transparent commerce applies particularly well to products that do not have mass market appeal. Niche product manufacturers can become online retailers by publicizing themselves on the internet to establish direct contact with their customers. Likewise, new customers can find them more easily because of the internet's extensive searching capabilities.

Electronic shopping can also be facilitated by "intelligent agents," search engines that scan the internet for products and services that match a customer's requirements. This applies to niche products as well as mass market products. For example, a prototype agent developed by Andersen Consulting, "Bargain Finder," searched the internet for compact discs, and compared prices to identify the best buy.

In all of these cases, the key to success is the customer's ability to access extensive information. Wherever mass market online retailers can effectively utilize the internet's capacity to offer in-depth information about products and services, they may even be able to outperform conventional retail. In this category, books, wine, computers, and software are already being sold successfully.

Another area in which online retail may have impact is in repetitive retail purchasing. Peapod, based in Chicago and operating in a number of other U.S. cities including San Francisco, offers a grocery shopping service that accepts orders through a product database that is accessible on the internet. A Peapod employee then gathers the products from a local retail grocery store and delivers them to the home for a modest service fee. For the customer, the saving is time, but for the local retail affiliates of Peapod, one of the key advantages is that the model builds customer loyalty even though the customer never has to come into the store.

b. Fee for service is a promising area for internet commerce, since any kind of service that has significant underlying information or knowledge content has good potential. The opportunities will be even stronger when the information is time-sensitive, making constant updates and immediate access very important.

Consequently, many time-based information services that are available through conventional media are migrating to the internet to take advantage of the internet's low cost of entry and global access to new customers.

Companies that offer classified advertising, employment advertising, dating services, and access to research databases are all exploring the internet's potential, as these kinds of matching functions can utilize the capacity for detailed information as well as constant updating.

3.   Business to business commerce

a. The extranet. There is great potential for business to business commerce to become a significant aspect of the internet. Since wholesale commerce separates purchasing decisions from the transaction and delivery, and since many business to business transactions are repetitive, the entire process can be highly automated.

As a complement to the intranet for internal communications, this form of commerce is now being referred to as the "extranet."

Wal-Mart has pioneered this kind of commerce, and the company's success has stimulated a worldwide movement toward direct connections between suppliers and distributors. For a decade, these relationships have fallen into the domain of Electronic Data Interchange, or EDI, but now that the internet has become an inexpensive and universal network medium, EDI business is migrating to extranets.

To capitalize on and support this transition, Netscape and General Electric Finance have formed a joint venture, Actra, to develop and market standardized extranet software.

b. Business information. Another potentially important business to business application of the internet is in business information. There are already many companies offering internet access to proprietary databases that contain news, demographics, and research, and this trend will continue strongly. It is likely that new businesses will emerge to offer more customized services that move beyond data and information toward knowledge, understanding, and wisdom.

In addition, because the internet is unaffected by distances between people, it offers the possibility of being a medium for customized knowledge work to be commissioned and delivered, particularly in time-critical situations.

We visualize this by imagining that a leading business consultant or scholar such as Peter Drucker can be commissioned online to analyze your particular business problem. He sends his advice back to you in a couple of hours over the internet. This "Peter Drucker Channel" thus offers direct access to the knowledge services of a world-class thinker. The price, no doubt, will be high, but obtaining the right analysis and insight at the right time makes the cost irrelevant.

4. Gambling and gaming will probably be big businesses on the internet. Gambling is a worldwide addiction, and in the U.S. revenue from state-run lotteries is rising 10% annually, while revenue from private video poker is growing 17% annually.[19]

Since the internet is a global medium, local and even national government control will be largely ineffective. Attempts to regulate or shut down an online casino merely prompts the gambling house to move elsewhere.

Competitive adventure games that are not particularly oriented to gambling will also thrive on the internet, including multi-player fantasy games that have been a staple of internet culture since long before the world wide web was created.

5.  Programming content
    a.  News
    b.  Customized news
    c.  Entertainment
    d.  Education

Programming content provided through the internet moves this medium towards the broadcasting model, regardless of whether the content is news or entertainment. As we have noted above, some broadcast organizations are offering their news feeds through web sites, including Fox, CNN and NBC.

In contrast with broadcast news, the internet is uniquely able to support customized services, such as reports that users craft to their own specific interests using standardized tool kits in a hybrid push-pull format. It is not clear if services like this will be commercially viable, but certainly a lot of attempts are already being made to develop this market because the potential for advertising revenue is so large.

Another approach to customized news is the online newsletter that is compiled and distributed in real time to vertical markets. Due the power of online data gathering, a publisher can compile and edit a tremendous scope and depth in minimal time with minimal staff. For certain kinds of business customers, these services could command premium prices.

A great amount of educational content is already available online, as institutions worldwide are actively looking for new places to sell the curricula materials that they have invested so much to develop. The possibilities for reaching new students who do not live nearby is a strong attraction.

For students who wish to engage in remote learning, there will be an increasing number of options to choose from. Remote learning will be particularly relevant for highly specialized subjects, which should now be able to attract larger student groups as geographical boundaries will be overcome electronically. Specialized medical education and diagnosis is already being done online.

6.   Directories

   a.  Of people and organizations (white & yellow pages)

   b.  Maps

   c.  Guides (restaurant, club, movie, etc.)

   d.  Matching services

The business of online directories is already established, with local, national, and international organizations competing in this field.

Their success will depend on whether or not the internet attracts a true critical mass of users who become accustomed to using this medium in the way that people are now accustomed to using the phone book.

In France, the Minitel replaced the phone book in the 1980s and created the world's first nation-wide online community medium, one which is now fully integrated into French culture. The internet represents challenging competition for the minitel, and it will force France Telecom to adapt to accommodate the internet, the tool that has become the world's online community medium.

Matching services will function much like shopping services, but with the focus not on facilitating a purchase, but on establishing connections between people who shares needs and interests.

7.   Marketing

   a.  Branding and image management

   b.  Personalized advertising

An area with the great potential for internet commerce is in marketing. With the capacity to search millions of web sites for particular words or phrases, the oft-used search engines turn every word, and essentially every name, into a brand.

This is the marketer's dream fulfilled, because it puts a premium on the capacity to communicate effectively with customers through knowledge-based marketing and design skills. The need to design rich, interactive web sites as promotional tools is also a nightmare, however, for the skills required to do this work are no longer available cheaply. Further, the standards of acceptable design are evolving rapidly, and yesterday's hot web site may already be passé today.

The need to market on the internet is exacerbated where the target audience is people aged 15−35. They are the majority of web users, and their ability to mercilessly critique a web site is legendary. For marketers of products and services directed at these markets, a presence on the internet has become a necessary accompaniment to television advertising as a tool for developing and managing brands.

However, the dynamics of internet marketing are different from other media. The linear and sequential mass media of publishing, radio, and television use the broadcast paradigm to enable producers and distributors to control content that is provided in finished form to the recipients.

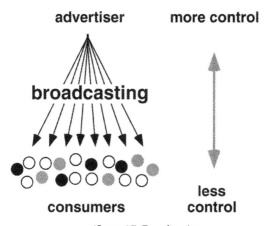

(figure 15) Broadcasting

In contrast, successful pull advertising on the web is not advertising in the conventional sense of the term, but rather interactive communications that must have a high knowledge content to attract attention. The world wide web is omnidirectional, simultaneous, and users navigate themselves wherever they want to go. This shifts the locus of control to users who craft their own experiences to an unprecedented degree, having the capability to select the content and specify the timing of its delivery. This new paradigm has been labeled "personalcasting," or, as suggested by Lawrence Wilkinson of Global Business Network, "narrowcatching."

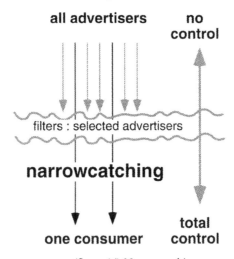

(figure 16) Narrowcatching

While the economics of broadcasting are based on revenue from advertising that accompanies content delivery, narrow- catchers can filter out any or all advertising, thereby disabling the critical revenue stream of the advertising industry and disrupting a system that has evolved over the last half century.

As control shifts to users, the passive character of television viewing is displaced by the interactive experience of browsing, and since browsing is a kind of learning, this means that the one-dimensional nature of passive televised entertainment is being displaced by a many-dimensional learning process.

Thus, while the broadcast and push paradigms will persist as a mass process of building brand names through sheer repetition, the narrowcatching model will enable individual consumers to gain access to critical knowledge whenever they wish to do so.

There are early indications that the popularity of narrowcatching is shifting the balance between television and the internet. Among the relatively small population of intense internet users there are already persistent stories of less television viewing, and according to Forrester Research, 80% of PC users report that they have reduced their television viewing time.[20]

This is another reason that broadcast networks are experimenting with video feeds to their web sites, as they chase former customers who are drifting to other pastimes.

If this trend continues and the internet displaces television as a preferred entertainment and learning medium, there will be radical shifts in the advertising industry and the broadcasters that they support. This reinforces the growing importance of the internet as a "knowledge channel."

## The knowledge channel

When we position the seven types of internet applications that we have described above on the information industry map, it is apparent that they are located along the top and right sides, clustering toward the upper right corner.

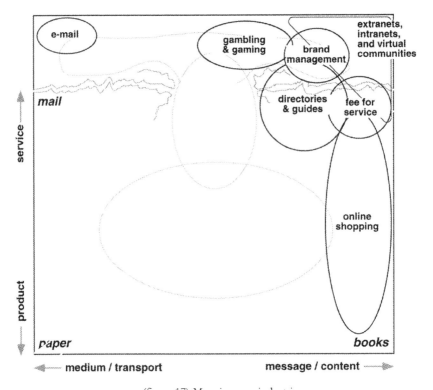

(figure 17) Mapping new industries

Again, this reflects one of the defining characteristics of the knowledge economy, the need for detailed information about products and services. As the act of consumption becomes a process of co-creation between producers and consumers, consumers must learn more about the products and services that are available so they can make the best choices.

This new and continually expanding requirement for information is leading companies to implement a new form of communications channel to complement the traditional distribution channels for products and services, the "knowledge channel."[21]

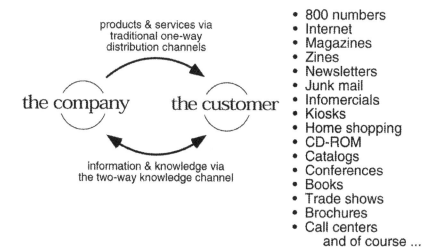

the company    the customer

products & services via
traditional one-way
distribution channels

information & knowledge via
the two-way knowledge channel

- 800 numbers
- Internet
- Magazines
- Zines
- Newsletters
- Junk mail
- Infomercials
- Kiosks
- Home shopping
- CD-ROM
- Catalogs
- Conferences
- Books
- Trade shows
- Brochures
- Call centers
    and of course ...
- The sales force

(figure 18) The two channels

During the last decade, companies have recognized and responded to this need with tools such as toll-free 800 phone numbers for customer feedback and questions. Today it is rare to find a consumer product that does not have an 800 number printed on the label.

But toll free telephone numbers have high costs and limited utility. In contrast, the internet offers tremendous potential for the knowledge channel because it can easily accommodate a tremendous quantity of information in nearly any format, and web sites can make the necessary information accessible on demand directly from large databases.[22]

As more and more people use the internet, the cost per person to provide a very high quality of information online declines dramatically in comparison with the cost of traditional media.

At a minimum, a portion of the printing budget can be shifted to the development of internet web sites, offering the advantage that web-based information can be updated very easily and without the necessity of reprinting brochures or the pain of throwing away outdated ones.

Some companies are already exploiting this potential. Rollerblade's web site, for example, promotes rollerblading culture, and also offers detailed information about the company's products and their use. There are even short video clips that detail safety and maintenance procedures.

Here we see that when detailed knowledge is available at the same time that community building happens, internet commerce takes on new and possibly important dimensions, as this could become a marketplace whose context is defined by the diverse needs of many different kinds of communities. It is clear, then, that the knowledge channel is also located at the upper right corner of the information industry map.

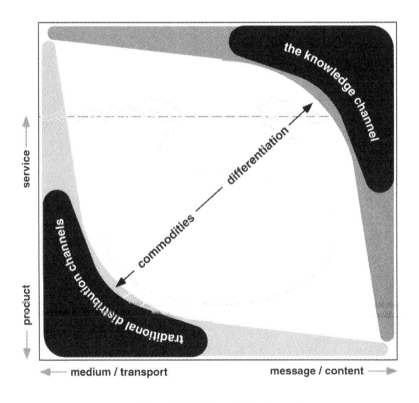

(figure 19) The knowledge channel

In addition, as information technology is integrated into products, they become more complex and require more knowledge to operate. This creates the need for more product-related information and instruction, and at the same time these products gain the capacity to become part of a networked world, to exchange messages with other systems and devices. Hence, it is clear that the internet is evolving into a network that connects not only people using computers, but devices communicating with other devices. This makes it easier for users to grasp and utilize complex functions by giving them the knowledge they require precisely when it is needed, at the point of use.

A final point about the knowledge channel. When we overlay the path to wisdom on the information business map, the domain of knowledge is found in the upper right corner, while the domains of understanding and wisdom lie, for the moment, beyond the competence of the map. It is there, perhaps, that entrepreneurs of the next century may find new opportunities.

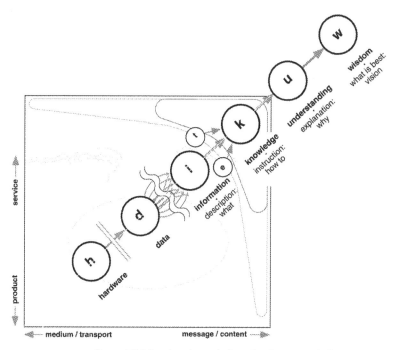

(figure 20) Mapping the path from hardware to wisdom

During the Age of Exploration these uncharted portions of the map might have been labeled "Here Be Dragons," and while we no longer believe in dragons, we also don't know much more about the unknown territory of understanding and wisdom than they did five hundred years ago.

For today, nevertheless, it is clear that great opportunities exist to add value by using the internet as the channel through which to fulfill the growing need for knowledge, while the search for understanding and wisdom continues.

# *4 Implications For Corporate Strategy*

There is little doubt that the evolving internet mass medium has strategic implications for companies in nearly every industry. It is likely to impact not only on external relations with customers, on internal management practices, but just as importantly on how we all think about the world.

The immanence of such fundamental change makes it very desirable to have a clear picture of what is likely to happen, but achieving this is deeply problematic.

For example, in 1983 AT&T hired McKinsey & Company to assess the future of cellular telephone market. Since the prediction was off by more than 2000%, the business decisions that AT&T made as a result ended up costing the company billions of dollars.[23](figure 21)

Whether it is the technologists themselves who make the forecasts or the consulting firms that they hire, things often go differently than predicted. (figure 22)

As a result of the persistently dismal track record, some consultants prefer the blanket prediction that, "All predictions are wrong." While this is convenient for the futurists, it is not particularly helpful for executives. Since every decision is also a prediction, executives are obliged to make predictions as a regular part of their daily work.

But it takes time to gather complete information, and while waiting to make a decision the market environment may be rapidly changing. Windows of opportunity open and close, and in any case the choice not to make a decision is itself a decision, and possibly a significant one.

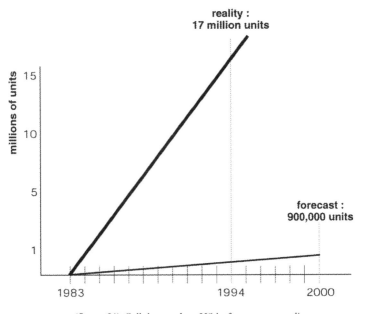

(figure 21) Cellular market, USA, forecast vs. reality


**"This 'telephone' has too many**
**shortcomings to be seriously considered**
**as a means of communication.  The device**
**is inherently of no value to us."**
Western Union
1876


**"Everything that can be invented**
**has been invented."**
C.H. Duell
US Commissioner of Patents 1899


**"There is no reason anyone would want a**
**computer in their home."**
Ken Olsen, Founder
Digital Equipment Corp.
1977

(figure 22) Some predictions by inside experts

# A structural model of economic change

So while precious few may be able to predict specific events particularly well, it will probably be more useful to look at the patterns that underlie the events. In the transition from the industrial economy of the 19th and 20th centuries to the knowledge economy of the 21st, one of the most compelling patterns is the enormous impact of new technologies on established markets, particularly during the last 25 years.

A good example is the credit card industry, which was created in large part by American Express. Throughout the 20th century, the company developed a global communications network and unique services for which it could charge premium prices. By the 1970s, however, the global infrastructure of telecommunications and the parallel development of large scale computing caught up with Amex and enabled Visa to become a significant competitor.

Visa pursued a strategy of ubiquity and low cost, and by consistently exploiting its unique position as a joint venture among banks and its use of new technology, the company was able to transform the differentiated market that American Express dominated into a commodity market whose key characteristic was price.

In the two decades following the rise of Visa, American Express struggled to understand the behavior of its new competition, and to respond to it. When it was clear in 1993 that CEO James Robinson could not come to grips with the scale and scope of changes in the marketplace, he was abruptly fired by the Amex Board of Directors.

The same process seems to apply to many other industries as well. In the personal computer industry, Apple saw the advantages of its Macintosh eroded by the progress of Windows, but failed to respond. In the end, the differentiated Mac market was swept into the commodity market defined by the Windows-Intel alliance, crushing Apple's profit margins in the process.

In the auto industry, the Japanese turned the differentiated luxury car into a commodity by mastering the efficient design and manufacture of high quality cars. Lexus, Acura, and Infiniti displaced Cadillac, Mercedes, and BMW at the pinnacle of the market.

In these situations it is clear that the application of new technology may have compelling impact on existing differentiated markets. In particular, the use of information technology spreads know-how, enabling new competitors to enter the market. Further, new technology can make it possible to offer high quality products and services at lower cost, enabling newcomers to undercut the cost basis of existing providers.

Third, technology can reduce the underlying cost of administration and management, leaving companies with high operating cost structures trapped in marginal market niches.

Finally, technology can redefine the competitive game by switching who controls whom in the chain of value.

Separately or together, the result is a pattern whereby industries and industry segments that once supported product or service differentiation and premium pricing lose that advantage to new competitors who cleverly apply new knowledge and new technologies to create new market niches. Once-differentiated companies find themselves thrust into commodity markets where they have no protection, and where they are forced to fight for identity and market share.

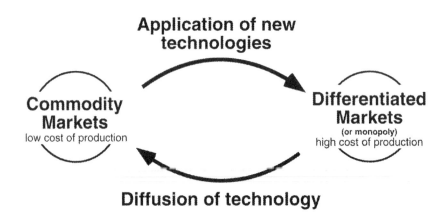

(figure 23) The diffusion of technology as a driver of economic change

Harvard professor Michael Porter defined the terminology of differentiation and commodity strategies, but apparently he has not extended his analysis to show how technology drives change as a general process.[24] This dynamic effect of technology seems to be one of the major forces that is displacing the industrial model and creating the knowledge age, a process that largely explains the massive discontinuities in the marketplace and the board room that we have observed during the last fifteen years.

The same dynamic is clearly present when regulated monopolies are deregulated. Because of their monopoly protection, they enjoy premium pricing and sustain themselves profitably as high cost producers. When their monopoly protection is removed, however, valuable knowledge is disseminated throughout the market and they are forced to compete with low cost producers in commodity markets.

Many of the hundreds of thousands of people who lost their jobs in the massive layoffs of the early 1990s worked in industries where this dynamic was prevalent. High cost producers found themselves unable to compete in the new commodity markets in which they unexpectedly found themselves: In the telephone industry following the breakup of AT&T; in the computer industry with the shift to the client-server architecture; in the airline industry following its deregulation; and coming soon to an electric utility near you.

But it wasn't just the rank and file who lost their jobs. In a prior work, *Managing the Evolving Corporation*, I compiled a list of 16 CEOs of major American companies who were fired between 1991 and 1993.[25]

| | | |
|---|---|---|
| American Express | James Robinson III | January 1993 |
| Ames Department Stores | Stephen L. Pistner | December 1992 |
| Apple | John Sculley | July 1993 |
| Compaq | Rod Canion | October 1991 |
| Cyprus Minerals | Chester B. Stone | February 1992 |
| Digital | Kenneth Olsen | October 1992 |
| GM | Robert Stempel | October 1991 |
| Goodyear | Tom Barrett | June 1991 |
| Hartmarx | Harvey A. Weinberg | July 1992 |
| Imcera Group | M. Blakeman Ingle | December 1992 |
| IBM | John Akers | January 1993 |
| Kodak | Kay Whitmore | October 1993 |
| R.H. Macy | Edward S. Finkelstein | April 1992 |
| Sunbeam/Oster | Paul B. Kazarian | January 1993 |
| Tenneco | James B. Ketelson | May 1992 |
| Westinghouse | Paul Lego | Janaury 1993 |

(figure 24) 16 fired CEOs, 1991—1993

Reviewing that list from the perspective of differentiated and commodity markets, it is apparent that at least ten of the fired CEOs (including James Robinson of Amex) were caught in the economic discontinuity brought on by technology.

From this I concluded that most of these fired CEOs must have misunderstood the nature of the challenges that they faced. They apparently failed to realize that they had encountered not just another business cycle, but a fundamental and permanent change in the character of their industries, one that was largely driven by the diffusion of new technology.

This situation has led to a significant change in how future CEOs are identified. Whereas it was once the case that future CEOs were developed within a corporation, and succession plans were carefully implemented over decades, it has now become common for the insiders to be passed over. Today, 40 of the largest 100 American corporations are run by CEOs who were recruited from the outside.[26]

This says in no uncertain terms that being on the inside is not necessarily an advantage, and it may be a tremendous disadvantage. As the rate of change accelerates, it may become more difficult for insiders to recognize the important trends, to understand their meaning, and to make the necessary and difficult adjustments to corporate culture and corporate strategy that they demand.

Hence, corporate boards are now looking outside for new ideas, new experiences, new business models, and experience with new technologies to reinvigorate their organizations.

As a new technology that is becoming a mass market, the internet has the potential to amplify these dynamics in many existing industries, and force an even faster rate of change. We have already discussed possible impacts on broadcasting, advertising, television and computer manufacturing, and while we don't have high expectations for internet retail in the short term, over the long term it will displace distributors and retailers in many market segments.

To prepare for these kinds of challenges, our extension of Porter's model suggests that there are four strategic platforms, four generalized business models to employ depending upon the company, the industry, and the underlying trends:

1. Applying new technology to strip away differentiation
2. Competitive strategies for established commodity markets
3. Applying new technologies to create differentiation
4. Adding value to sustain differentiation

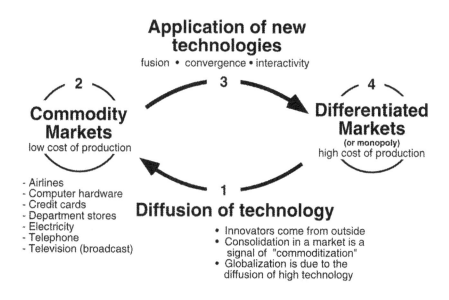

(figure 25) The diffusion of technology as a driver of economic change

The use of these strategies is not mutually exclusive, nor is it even black and white. It is not unusual for a company to apply more than one strategy and more than one platform at the same time, even in the same market segment. Nevertheless, the model will be useful if it helps to focus on the correct patterns rather than just on the confusion of events. It also provides an interesting tool for reverse engineering the strategies of competitors, suppliers, and customers that one needs to understand more clearly.

1. Diffusion of technology

Companies that master new technologies may be able to apply that knowledge to strip away the protection that their competitors formerly enjoyed. This transforms markets that once supported differentiation into commodity markets that are highly price sensitive.

There seem to be four ways for this kind of transition to be forced:

a. Applying technology to speed up critical processes

b. Developing new, lean cost models

c. Using technology to control critical market segments, and

d. Managing complexity more effectively.

We have already discussed how Hewlett Packard uses a fast development cycle in the home computer market, and how Chrysler and other cars companies have reduced the time it takes to develop new cars from 84 to 30 months. Another example of speed is Federal Express, whose overnight delivery business is built on an impressive technological infrastructure that optimizes reliability.

Some companies use technology to develop lean cost structures, enabling them to sell products and services that once commanded premium prices at commodity prices. Visa is an example of this, as are Dell Computer, MCI, Southwest Airlines, and Wal-Mart.

In many cases, these newcomers have significant advantages over companies that have been around for a long time because the new ones can implement frugal cost models more easily. Older competitors are bound by history, by old ways of working, by labor agreements, and by obsolete technology. Hence, while it may have been necessary to Apple's survival for the company to license the Mac operating system to Power Computing, Motorola, and Supermac, the price in the short term is competitors that are stronger than Apple in some market segments because their costs are lower. Many of the 4100 people that Apple laid off in early 1997 are certainly casualties of this phenomenon.

Companies such as Microsoft and Intel control markets by controlling critical technology. Since all PC applications work on Intel chips and Microsoft operating systems, IBM gave its former suppliers control of a huge segment of the computer industry. Likewise, American Airlines controls the Sabre travel reservations system, which acts as a gatekeeper to a large portion of the travel industry.

The fourth strategy that turns differentiated markets into commodities is a consequence of the management of complexity. Companies such as Fujitsu, Glaxo, NEC, and Chase Manhattan use their capacity to manage very complex situations to reduce the cost of doing business.

At Chase, for example, a critical cost factor is credit card fraud. The company therefore developed artificial intelligence software to identify possible instances of fraud. The software examines 50 million transactions at a time using computers that manipulate terabytes of data, and when these systems were first used in the early 1990s they provided Chase with a distinctive cost advantage. Since then, however, the systems that Chase developed have been successfully replicated by its competitors, further driving the entire industry deeper into commodity dynamics.

NEC, Fujitsu, and Glaxo also have significant capabilities in the development and deployment of new technologies, which enable them to reduce their operating costs in areas such as new drug identification and development in the case of Glaxo, and new computer development at NEC.

The internet has enormous potential to affect all of these areas. By enabling producers and consumers to be in direct contact with one another, the speed of commerce is being dramatically accelerated, the overall cost of many transactions can be dramatically reduced, and high levels of complexity are being managed more easily.


2. Managing in commodity markets

When commodity pricing is irrevocable, another set of strategies come to the forefront. These include looking for innovation outside, consolidation into larger companies, globalization, and control of dominant designs.

When most of the innovations come from outside, it is an indication that insiders are trapped in old views of their businesses and are vulnerable to new thinking. The innovative Southwest Airlines, for example, was founded not by an airline industry veteran, but by a lawyer who saw an opportunity and a business model that insiders were blind to. Twenty-five years later,

Southwest is the only airline to be consistently profitable, and to receive consistently high satisfaction ratings from its customers.

Similarly, the Japanese auto manufacturers won a significant share of the American market beginning in the 1970s because the American manufacturers did not recognize that there was a large unfulfilled need for innovation and quality. Likewise, they were not ready for the quality and price wars that nearly put Ford and Chrysler out of business.

With 40 of the top 100 American companies being run by outsiders today, it is clear that new thinking is being widely sought across the economy.

Another signal of inexorable commodity conditions is rampant consolidation. Market share warfare has taken over, and companies acquire their competitors in order to capture new customers. This kind of competition has been described in classical economics as the struggle of declining returns. The total size of the market is permanently limited, and survival is a matter of fighting for market share.

Wal-Mart is a preeminent company using this strategy. It is now the largest retailer in the U.S., and is rapidly spreading its operations throughout South America and Asia. Likewise, America Online has become dominant among internet service providers by achieving the largest market share, which was obtained in a multi-year marketing blitz that was too successful. The company almost imploded on its growing membership and was forced to put its effective campaign on hold.

A third strategy for the commodity phase is linked to globalization. When the capacity to build or operate sophisticated equipment is not limited to a single market or region, competition becomes omnidirectional and new companies can invade any market from anywhere. This increases the pressure to keep prices as low as possible.

Another commodity market strategy is to control the dominant design or the key intellectual property in a segment. Perhaps the best high-tech example of a dominant design strategy is Microsoft, whose Windows product dominates the market even though its performance is not the best. Disney has achieved dominance in a key entertainment niche by creating, controlling, and successfully exploiting its own fictional characters.

The internet will also play a role in shaping commodity markets. Because it is so easy for "outsiders" to establish a presence on the internet, no established business is immune from competition. Further, a one-person company can look as impressive on the world wide web as a giant multinational, blurring the nature of competition even more.

In addition, the internet as a knowledge channel brings new intellectual property to a wide market and can rapidly overturn an existing dominant design. Barnes and Noble, established more than a century ago with more than 100 stores and $2.45 billion in annual sales, is suddenly threatened by tiny Amazon.com, 2 years old, no stores, and less than $20 million in annual sales.

## 3. Moving toward differentiation

The third major strategy area is the application of new methods and technologies to escape the restraints of commodity markets. This is the domain in which innovation is a key competitive factor, as exemplified by companies such as Sun Microsystems, Sony, and Saturn.

Whereas innovations that pertain to internal cost structures deepen the commodity trench, innovations that are visible to customers in the form of improvements to products and services can create new differentiation that helps companies to move out of the commodity stage.

These innovations may pertain to the design of the product, or they may involve innovations in service, the process of manufacturing or delivery, or in management itself. Few of Saturn's innovations, for example, are in the car. Instead, most of them are managerial innovations that pertain to the processes of selling and servicing as it is experienced by the customer.

Since the differentiating value of many innovations erodes quickly, successful innovators require not just one innovation, but a constant stream to avoid being dragged back into the commodity fray.

Another way to escape the commodity trap is by exploiting new media. Netscape, Visa, CNN, and Chase are all examples of this. By using the new medium of artificial intelligence and mainframe computers to reduce fraud, Chase differentiated itself; Visa has done so through its global telecommunications system. Likewise, by exploiting existing communications satellites and the delivery medium of cable TV, CNN has become a global force in the news industry.

Netscape's core product, the web browser, is an unhesitant commodity that is given away for free to individuals, but the company successfully exploits its knowledge of this new medium by selling related server products to the developers of web sites.

An important source of differentiation through media concerns the social aspects of technology rather than the technology itself. The successful use of new media depends largely on the ability to understand the social dynamics that they create, particularly the kinds of communities that emerge around their use.

As we have noted, these dynamics are both specific and unique on the net. In particular, the internet enables companies to participate as members of online communities, but here the shift from supply-driven to demand-driven markets is clear, for here the rules are established by the participants, the customers, rather than by the companies. This is just one of the new and possibly difficult surprises that awaits established companies as they venture online.

### 4. Sustaining premium value

The fourth market is that in which differentiated advantage is sustainable on an (apparently) long term basis. There are essentially three ways by which this is done: service, design, and brand management.

Some companies offer better service and can charge higher prices as a result. Federal Express may be the best example of this, as they receive 50 times more revenue per package than the Post Office for about the same service. Nordstrom and Charles Schwab also differentiate themselves by the quality of their service. Schwab has developed a clever and complex niche, in that the company uses a high quality of service to differentiate itself in the business of offering discounted stock brokerage services.

Some companies create and defend their advantages through design, among them Nike, Sony, Disney, and Braun. The products and the packaging promote the image of the company and reinforce a consistent marketing message.

Interestingly, Nike, Sony, and Disney have all migrated towards full control of the environment as well as the product. Nike has created its elaborate and very successful NikeTown stores, which have quickly became leading tourist attractions, while Sony also has its own showcase stores and Disney has created retail stores to diffuse the message defined in its successful amusement parks (where control is taken to extremes).

Finally, some companies are extraordinarily good at brand management, and they use their brands to sustain differentiated advantage. Microsoft and Boeing are prime examples of successful companies that are sustained by tremendous public relations successes even though their products are in many ways inferior to the competition.

Companies that emphasize design also tend to focus on brand management, and Nike, Disney, and Sony all do this very well, as does Proctor and Gamble, which is considered a premier "training school" for brand managers.

Even Intel now seeks differentiation through its "intel inside" branding, even though no one expects most customers to ever see a Pentium chip.

## Increasing returns

The differentiated market-commodity market model is complemented by another useful model, one that helps define the differences between industrial age industries and knowledge age industries.

In contrast to the declining returns that are characteristic of industrialized commodity markets, some differentiated markets create what economist Brian Arthur has identified as "increasing returns."[27] Increasing returns are evident in knowledge markets when the very success of a foundation technology, product, or product family itself creates a market that increases in size as more people are drawn to participate.

Since the incremental cost to serve new customers is almost insignificant, the growth of the market is not constrained by the availability of or the cost dynamics of natural resources.

Knowledge, not resources, is the critical factor in these markets, and knowledge is not used up when it is shared. In fact, it often becomes more valuable when it is shared, so the behavior of a community or network of users who share knowledge often leads to the positive feedback cycle of sustained growth.

When this happens. competing approaches are effectively "locked out" of the market, as the accepted approach attains a committed user base that is unable or unwilling to change.

This is precisely what is already occurring with the internet. As it grows and more people get on line, more providers are drawn to internet commerce to exploit the growing customer base. More services available on line draws more potential customers, and with this positive feedback cycle internet use continues to expand. Hence, we see Lotus shift its Notes product onto the internet, and Intuit abandons its proprietary financial network scheme just as EDI becomes the extranet.

However, Arthur warns that technology advances in waves, and increasing returns cycles endure only until a wave is displaced by the next one, and open competition returns.

This does not seem likely to happen with the internet for the foreseeable future, largely because so many new technologies are using it as a foundation. Thus, as the internet continues to develop it will become the infrastructure of a new mass medium, a new example of increasing returns, and a new marketplace that transforms all existing ones.

As it does so it will impact on every existing company in every existing market, because a significant portion of internet growth will come at the expense of established companies and industries. But just as importantly, the internet will permanently change the way that strategy is conducted throughout the economy, even in resource-bound industries that remain subject too declining returns.

# 5 *The View Forward*

## The long term

The general characteristic of a differentiated market is that it is constrained in some significant way, either in terms of who can compete as a provider or who can participate as a consumer. In contrast, most commodity markets are wide open to new competitors. As a medium that is intensely, perhaps obsessively open, and one whose core dynamic facilitates communication, the internet is likely to increase the pressure on differentiated markets to become commodity markets. In fact, the ease of starting a company and doing business on the internet is already leading to new forms of competition and creating new commodity markets on a widespread basis.

For mass market products, therefore, the internet will not support premium pricing, but rather discounting will be the norm. Amazon.com offers a 40% discounts, which it can afford to do precisely because its use of "back office" technology and "just in time" inventory has crushed operating costs to unprecedented lows.

Hence, it is clear that to sustain differentiation when market forces are driving towards commoditization, it is necessary to develop and exploit knowledge channel strategies that constantly advance the possibilities for adding the highest value.

In this context, McKinsey consultants John Hagel and Arthur Armstrong make a revealing comment in their book *net gain*. They note that manufacturers and vendors generally enjoy "information advantages" over their customers because they know more about their products and services than customers do.[28]

As a medium through which that information advantage is eroded or eliminated entirely, the internet catalyzes a shift of power away from corporations and back to individual customers. Therefore, the only way to succeed in this environment is to participate willingly, to provide customers with high levels of useful knowledge.

As we have already discussed, the "Peter Drucker Channel" is a premium consulting service strategy that will offer unprecedented value and command unheard of pricing. At the other extreme, hardware manufacturers will continue to struggle with the forces of commoditization.

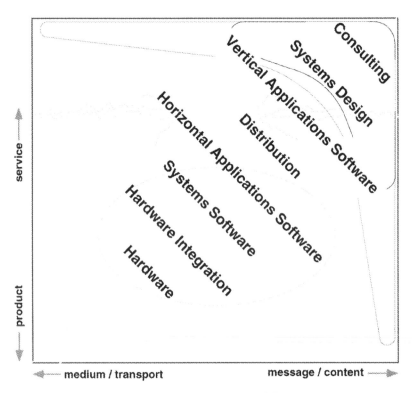

(figure 26) From commodity to differentiation

This process can also be generalized by reference to the path to wisdom. Each advance in the evolution of the marketplace moves the kinds of products and services that are treated as commodities further to the right.

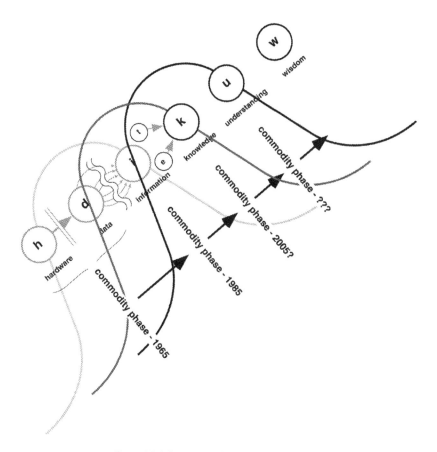

(figure 27) The commoditization of the marketplace

With the first computers, even data was bought at a differentiated price. Rapid competition in the computer marketplace was driven by chip improvements, and resulted in unprecedented performance increases and price reductions. Robert Reich points out that in 1984, 80% of the cost of a computer was in the hardware, while by 1990 only 20% was in hardware and the rest was software.[29]

Today, it is not only data, but also information, that have become commodities.

Largely due to the influence of technology, we are now seeing commodity pressure on knowledge-related activities and products, so clearly the bell curve of economic activity is shifting further to the right.

As a medium for the sharing of knowledge, the internet is a key force driving the commoditization of knowledge on a global basis. Hence, the farther to the right a product or service lies on the model, the longer it will be able to sustain differentiation, and the more effectively it can be packaged and sold. The more understanding (the "why") and wisdom (the vision) that is embedded and expressed in a product or service, the higher the market will tend to value it, and for this reason we are particularly interested in the knowledge channel.

## The short to medium term

Over the short to medium term, the internet is being shaped by these forces:

A.   The social phenomenon of internet use by rapidly increasing numbers of people

B.   The continuing development of the internet's technical infrastructure

C.   The impact of governmental regulation

D.   The extent to which the internet push technology enables the internet to become a hybrid broadcast-narrowcatch medium

E.   The expansion of internet commerce, particularly in areas other than conventional retail

A. The social phenomenon.

Regardless of its commercial development, the Internet will have increasing influence on the social process of human communications, and the continuing expansion of internet use by more people is already significant. According to Nielson Media Research, 50 million people in North America used the internet at least once during December, 1996, up from 19 million earlier that year.[30]

The ease by which individuals who share an interest can form themselves into a group is unprecedented. Since they can easily be located by others who share the same interest, the many-to-many character of internet dialog is explosive.

Through this process, the very character of social dialog itself may be evolving. The use of the internet as a communications tool for social and political movements has spread worldwide, and many feel an increased openness. In the words of journalist Jon Katz,

"On the Net last year, I saw the rebirth of love for liberty in media. I saw a culture crowded with intelligent, educated, politically passionate people who—in jarring contrast to the offline world—line up to express their civic opinions, participate in debates, even fight for their political beliefs. I watched people learn new ways to communicate politically. I watched information travel great distances, then return home bearing imprints of engaged and committed people from all over the world. I saw positions soften and change when people were suddenly able to talk directly to one another, rather than through journalists, politicians, or ideological mercenaries. I saw the primordial stirrings of a new kind of nation—the Digital Nation—and the formation of a new postpolitical philosophy." [31]

Indeed, the unique character of internet discourse has already prompted a member of the U.S. Congress to suggest that each American should be guaranteed access to the internet with a private account.

Online communities also create a method by which customers can participate in the development of the new economy, for by joining online dialogs in virtual communities, customers become the ultimate content providers. Steve Case, CEO of America Online put it this way in 1992: "Everybody will become information providers as well as consumers. The challenge is to create electronic communities that marry information and communications—thereby creating an interactive, participatory medium. The community aspect is crucial—it is the soul of the new medium." [32]

Some years and many millions of members later, America Online leads its rivals as medium of community and, increasingly, of commerce. If development continues along this path and everyone (or nearly everyone) gets online, then commerce will inevitably follow in full force. Eventually every product and service that can be obtained in any market, whether legitimate or illegal, will also be accessible on the internet.

B. The technical infrastructure.

The continuing development of the technical infrastructure, particularly through refinements to user interfaces and faster access speeds will accelerate the growth of the internet. When cable modems transmitting at 10 megabits per second become common, there will be new rage of enthusiasm for the many-to-many medium.

However, if the infrastructure fails to keep up with growing demand, and if users continue to endure long waits or encounter continuing reliability problems, then the development of the internet will be slower and may never achieve critical mass as an enduring social and commercial phenomenon. For the present, it seems that the internet infrastructure will successfully adapt to growing demand, but there will continue to be new technical obstacles to be dealt with in the coming decades.

C. Governmental regulation.

The impact of governmental regulation is significant for many new technologies, and it will continue to be the case with the internet. In areas such as free speech, pornography, privacy, cryptography, and the deployment of infrastructure, the government has significant influence on how quickly internet becomes embedded in modern culture.

An interesting comparison is the history of the fax machine, which was already in widespread use in Japan as early as the 1930s. The capacity to transmit images can be critical to communication in a language whose three alphabets have thousands of characters, but Japanese law restricted the use of fax machines to dedicated phone lines, making it illegal to transmit data over voice lines. Consequently, fax machines were used mostly by government bodies and large corporations.[33]

Forty years later, Japanese telecommunications law was changed to permit data transmissions over voice lines, which stimulated an overnight explosion of demand for fax machines. Adoption in the West lagged Japan by about 2 years, but the growth curves are nearly identical.

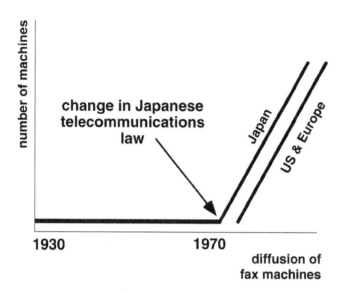

(figure 28) The impact of governmental regulation on the diffusion of technology

As the internet becomes more deeply embedded in society, it is evolving into a public utility as an extension of the phone system, and this will inevitably lead to the call for systematic regulation.

There are many ways that the government could restrict or attempt to restrict internet use, either by acts of congress or through rules issued by the executive branch. The social growth of the internet has strong application in politics, as the internet offers significant possibilities for communication with broad constituencies and special interest groups. Political parties may therefore be inspired to seize upon the internet as a political issue beyond their current obsession with pornography. These issues will be hotly debated at all levels in the coming years.


D. A broadcast – narrowcatch medium.

The initial development path of the internet led to the creation of a medium with characteristics far different than broadcasting. With the focus on scientific collaboration and interpersonal dialog, commercialism was shunned.

Thus, the initial wave of commercial interest in the internet was something of a setback to internet purists who valued their medium of dialog. However, commercialism became inevitable with the development of the world wide web and its graphic interface, and today the commercial and noncommercial aspects of the internet cohabitate quite readily.

As push technologies merge the broadcast television paradigm with the internet's information-based pull approach, the result will be a new mass medium with transformative potential. Together with the merger of the television and the PC, the influence on mainstream entertainment, news, marketing, and advertising will be decisive.

E. Commercial growth.

Commercial development is inexorably following the creation of new communities. People are becoming accustomed to buying products on the internet on a mass basis as the problems of interface, image display size, payment, and security are resolved. Over the long term, we expect a robust internet retail trade to be extensive, well established, and profitable in many market segments.

As a market in which to invest, the internet thus offers opportunities that will not be bound by the current limitations of internet retail. Many of these lie at the intersection of the social aspects of internet as a forum for building virtual communities and its power as a medium of knowledge building and knowledge exchange.

While direct retail sales will ultimately be a small proportion of internet revenues, the medium of the internet is ideally suited to sharing information and providing customized information and knowledge to match specific needs.

Hence, a significant proportion of internet revenues should come in areas such as:

a.   Matching functions

b.   Knowledge channel publishing

c.   Customized products and services

Many applications in these areas will use internet technology to transform formerly differentiated markets into commodity markets, and as such they offer new opportunities for entrepreneurs and investors.

a. Matching functions. The internet offers key strengths wherever there is a large database of time-sensitive information that must be searched in order to fill particular needs. Here, demand meets supply on an individual basis.

Since the internet resides entirely on computers, it is sensible to marry database capabilities with the inherent network functions of the internet.[34] In addition, information on a web site can be updated at any time, and remotely, so a matching database can evolve in real time. Third, since the internet is globally accessible, the pool of possible customers can be the largest possible size, i.e., everyone who is online.

Examples of this functionality include classified advertising for sales or purchases of products; offers of employment; pure and applied research; and services to match the skills of consultants and contract workers with the needs of employers.

b. Knowledge channel publishing will be a strong internet market, particularly for large volumes of information that are published on web sites and people are charged fees for access.

To date, the most prevalent application of this model has been pornography, but other applications of the same functionality are likely to become successful businesses.

As a knowledge channel, the internet appears to be fertile territory for advertisers, but since internet users are not captive viewers in the same way that television viewers are, the dynamics of internet advertising are different.

Consequently there are two predominant strategies for web advertising. First, there is the necessity and opportunity to build brand name recognition when customers see ads. As with the print advertising sector, the volume and quality of these impressions are the core of the "publisher's" billing process.

The internet offers additional capability in that web browsers can click on advertising banners to visit the web sites of advertisers. Those who "click through" should then arrive at a web site that is worth visiting because the right content is there and easy to find. This makes the design of a web site an important form of branding and advertising.

c. Customized products and services. An area in which the internet may be able to support a significant retail trade is customized products. By facilitating a direct link between manufacturers and buyers, the internet provides both with something that no other medium can match.

Customers benefit from direct access to manufacturers worldwide, while manufacturers have access to customers everywhere. The method of finding each other may be as simple as at few keystrokes on a search engine.

The internet will also be a good medium for products that are accompanied by extensive information, and for products that are information. What has been found in the first case, however, is that many people will retrieve information from the internet and then actually buy the product from a traditional source. Nevertheless, this offers manufacturers and retailers valuable opportunities to build brand recognition and to prepare sales that are consummated elsewhere.

## Summary: Barriers to entry and management strategy

As a medium of commerce in which the barriers to entry are low, the internet has drawn a wave of interest that has the feel of a gold rush, with companies racing to stake their claims in various niches of the new marketplace. One side effect of this is the feeling throughout the industry that the work of a full year is routinely compressed into only three months. Hence, one "normal year" is considered to be four "internet years."

How long this kind of effort can be sustained is a key question, but as long as an IPO waits at the end of the road, people will be motivated to push as hard as they can.

In such a dynamic environment, however, there is no way to keep up except by participating in the market on a day to day basis. Many of the vital qualities that make for a successful web site or internet-based company are emergent or intangible, and are very difficult to describe even though they can readily be seen and felt. The only way to understand these qualities is by experience, and therefore any firm that expects to participate in any aspect of internet commerce should establish a presence online as soon as possible in order to create a committed framework from which to learn about this new medium. Since the internet is having impact throughout the economy, this includes every company from You, Inc. to Exxon.

In the Introduction we suggested that there are seven key strategic issues presented this report, and while we hope that you have gotten a lot more than seven insights, we repeat them here as a summary of the crucial aspects of the internet as a matter of corporate strategy:

1    Paradigm change

The use of the internet at the leading edge of electronic dialog and electronic commerce will not be a short-lived phenomenon, but rather one that will endure as a significant factor in social and commercial life for many decades. One of the primary reasons for this is that the internet is the only mass medium yet to emerge that is fully coherent with the shift from the industrial economy to the knowledge age.

2    Critical mass

The growth of the internet since the invention of the World Wide Web in 1990 has been a sustained exponential process. In 1995, it was estimated that 10 million people used the internet. During 1996, this number grew to 20 million, and in 1997 it is estimated at 50 million. If current growth rates continue, by the year 2000 there will be between 300 and 400 million users. The positive feedback of network effects — that more people are drawn to participate as more people are participating — suggests that the actual numbers could very well be even higher, particularly if new, high-speed means of access such as cable modems become common.

3    The internet rupture

The evolution of the information industry from the 1970s through the 1990s is a story of dramatic growth. The rapid emergence of the internet during this decade has led, suddenly, to a rupture that is causing dislocations throughout the business world. Companies find their existing strategies imperiled, while at the same time the internet offers an abundance of new opportunities that must be considered.

## 4    The knowledge channel

As we observe a widespread shift from supply-driven markets to demand-driven markets, the individual comes to the fore as a learner and a consumer with increasing power in the marketplace. The internet is perhaps the ideal tool for communication with this new kind of customer through the "knowledge channel," direct linkages for sharing critical knowledge directly between producers and their customers, and among customers, in internet-based communities.

## 5    Internet communities

The internet is changing the dynamics of global society by enabling groups of like-minded individuals to form themselves into communities regardless of where they live. As communities share interests that may be related to companies and products, many of them will have significant commercial impact.

## 6    From differentiation to commodity

During the last twenty years, technology has been a force of change throughout the business world. To their surprise, many premium producers suddenly found themselves competing in commodity markets when innovative newcomers used technology to strip away their differentiated advantage.

The internet will be a catalyst of the same dynamic as the wide dispersion of knowledge will strip away the protection that many once-differentiated products and distribution channels formerly enjoyed.

An additional key factor driving commodity dynamics is that new technologies are emerging not in government and defense-related applications. Rather, consumer markets are now the key drivers of change as laboratories in which new technologies are perfected on a mass basis in an environment of highly concentrated learning.

## 7    Technology and strategy

As a consequence of all this, it is vital to take both a strategic view of the internet, and to use it in a strategic way to help position your company for the coming waves of competition. Business models must be carefully crafted to reflect the new structures and niches that electronic commerce is beginning to offer and will continue to offer in the coming years.

• • •

In this new marketplace, first-comers may have an advantage due to their early arrival, because this gives them the opportunity to build founding communities. These may create enduring links that will provide some protection against new and old competition. Entrepreneurs who understand the future first, and who respond adroitly to changing conditions, may also be able to establish dominant market presence (such as was the case with the Ford Model T).

Pioneers fail, on the other hand, when they are limited by shortages of capital or vision, and are unable therefore to benefit from their unique positions.

Sometimes they simply prepare the market for others who can better exploit the new possibilities that they create but cannot fulfill (such as IBM's dominance with mainframes and then the early PC).

The mass production and marketing of the automobile was an economic turning point that brought society fully into the industrial age; the emergence of computers marked the beginning of a fundamental change to an information-based society, and brought with it important new ways to operate in the "information business."

Hence, whether it is cars or computers, technology does change the way that business, and life, are conducted.

Today information technology represents one-sixth of our economy, and with the birth of the internet and its rapid growth, the knowledge economy is taking on new forms that are becoming socially and commercially important.

As we have discussed, the new economy and its new technologies are focused on how the knowledge of individuals is brought to society as a whole, and no medium has ever offered the potential to support this process on a global basis—until now.

# Appendix

Moore's 1st & 2nd Laws

In 1963, computer scientist Gordon Moore analyzed the short history of the computer chip and extrapolated forward to create a prediction that has come to be known as Moore's Law. Moore saw that competition in the chip industry was forcing manufacturers to continually design and produce more powerful chips in the quest for advantage in the marketplace. As a result, the processing capacity of the leading edge chip was doubled every two years, and Moore projected that this would continue for some time to come. A few years later it became clear that the rate of doubling was even faster than Moore had predicted, for the cycle time had been reduced to 18 months.

At the time, Moore expected the trend to taper off in the 1970s as the underlying laws of physics and the talents of chip engineers reached their natural limits. However, this did not happen. In fact, the pattern of doubling has continued to this day, now more than thirty years after Moore noticed the trend that bears his name.

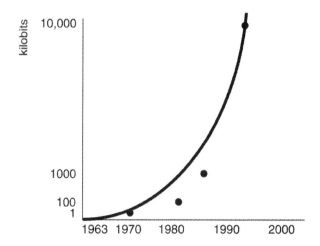

(figure 29) Moore's Law: The number of kilobits on a chip

79

In the history of commerce and technology, no similar trend has ever been sustained for so long, and with such astounding results. As a result of this compounding of performance, today's computer chips are thousands of times more powerful than those of the 1960s, and they make computer processing power available to tens of millions of people at a tiny fraction of its former cost.

|      |                       | MIPS | price        | $/MIPS      |
|------|-----------------------|------|--------------|-------------|
| 1975 | IBM mainframe         | 10   | $10,000,000  | $1,000,000  |
| 1976 | Cray 1                | 160  | $20,000,000  | $125,000    |
| 1979 | DEC VAX               | 1    | $200,000     | $200,000    |
| 1981 | IBM PC                | .25  | $3,000       | $12,000     |
| 1984 | Sun workstation       | 21   | $10,000      | $476        |
| 1994 | Pentium PC            | 66   | $3,000       | $45         |
| 1995 | Sony PCX video game   | 500  | $400         | $.80        |
| 1995 | Microunity set-top box| 1000 | $500         | $.50        |

(figure 30) Increasing MIPS—decreasing cost[35]

One side effect of this is that investors in the company that Moore cofounded in 1968, Intel, have done very well. And so has society in general. As processing power increases, it becomes economically feasible for more and more functions to be done by computers, and we have seen a steady stream of new applications for chips in each decade since the 60s.

Indeed, chips are so cheap and so useful for so many things that they are being used in every imaginable kind of product. Today, in fact, there are about 3 computer chips in "everyday" devices (a phenomenon known as "embedded computing") for every one that is used in an honest-to-goodness computer. In the coming years, chips will be embedded in furniture, clothing, shoes, walls, windows, doors, and just about everything else. As noted in Chapter 4, many of these chips will be linked to the internet, enabling devices to communicate with each other and with their users.

But whether or not the doubling trend underlying Moore's Law will continue for another three decades years is an open question. The scientists and engineers in the chip industry will have to overcome many technical obstacles, but they have succeeded in the past despite many doubters, including, at times, Moore himself.

There is another trend that may turn out to be just as important as Moore's Law, one that has to do with the cost of building the factories, or "fabs," in which computer chips are made. Moore himself has pointed out that the cost of a new fab also doubles with each generation of chips, a phenomenon that Forbes Magazine has dubbed "Moore's Second Law."

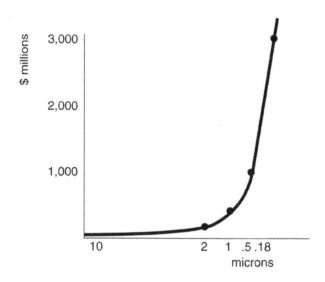

(figure 31) Moore's Second Law: The cost of a fab

Since every 18 months the industry moves from one generation of chip technology to the next, the pressure is tremendous to get new chips designed and manufactured. But it also takes two or three years to design a new chip and the fab in which it will be made, so the design-manufacture cycle is longer than the life cycle of the product in the market. Thus, a chip manufacturer has no way of recovering from a design failure, and in effect must bet the company on each subsequent generation of product.

Today's fabs cost in the range of $1 to $2 billion, and the sheer amount of capital that is required will force a structural change in the chip industry over the next decade. There will necessarily be a some form of consolidation or shakeout in the chip industry before 2005, even as the total market for chips continues to expand exponentially.

Already the signs are apparent. In 1997, National Semiconductor decided to close two of its chip manufacturing plants, build in the late 1980s, because they were "too old" to be effective. In most other industries, a ten year old plant would still be considered new.

Convergence

One of the most widespread applications of computer chip technology is in communications, the sending and receiving of messages electronically.

Most communications technologies used prior to the 1970s, including broadcast radio and television, cable radio and television, telephone, and microwave communications relied on analog signals whose amplitude and frequency carried encoded messages.

Beginning in the 1970s, engineers began applying digital computer technology to these various media to improve transmission quality, increase the transmission capacity of existing infrastructure, and to reduce the cost.

The telephone industry was the first to make the shift when engineers at AT&T's Bell Labs developed digital switching devices that could utilize AT&T's wire infrastructure much more efficiently than analog switching.

Bell Labs pioneered the science and technology of digital communications, which then spread to the radio, television, and wireless industries, in each case because the new applications offered higher quality and lower cost.

The unexpected side effect of this transition from analog to digital has been the convergence of all of these communications media towards a set of digital standards. Although the process is not yet complete, the foreseeable end point is the complete convergence of all of these formerly distinct communications technologies on a single set of standards that is applied to all digital forms of communication, resulting in near-total interconnectability.

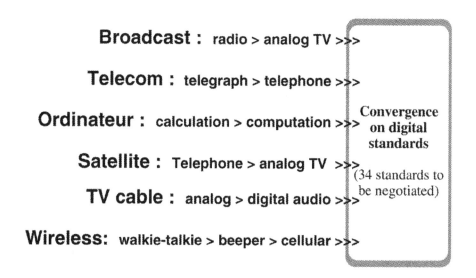

**Broadcast :** radio > analog TV >>>

**Telecom :** telegraph > telephone >>>

**Ordinateur :** calculation > computation >>>

**Satellite :** Telephone > analog TV >>>

**TV cable :** analog > digital audio >>>

**Wireless:** walkie-talkie > beeper > cellular >>>

Convergence
on digital
standards

(34 standards to
be negotiated)

(figure 32) Convergence

The technical challenges in this process are significant, and according to Robert Luff, formerly Chief Scientist of Scientific Atlanta, no fewer than 34 international standards must be agreed upon. The negotiation of each standard is laborious, but the potential benefits are so great that the process continues with the cooperation of representatives from government agencies and private industry worldwide.

When the possibility of convergence became widely apparent in the mid-1980s, executives of the seven local telephone companies (combined annual revenues, $80 billion) realized that they could use digital technology to compete with the cable television companies (combined annual revenues, $22 billion) by delivering TV signals to the homes of their customers over existing phone lines. Likewise, the cable companies saw that they could become phone companies by sending phone traffic over their TV cables. Both wanted to tap into the billions of dollars of new revenues that this possibility offered.

In addition, since digital signals require much less bandwidth because of compression technology such as MPEG, the cable operators would be able to expand from tens of channels to hundreds using their existing fiber and coaxial cable delivery infrastructure.

Further, and perhaps most interesting, the new converged technology offered the possibility of a higher level of interactivity than had ever existed before. With so much signal-carrying capacity in their transmission networks, integrated digital telephone and cable television systems had the potential to carry messages in both directions. Customers would be able to communicate back to the cable company to choose what they wanted to watch, and they would send the messages via their remote controls through the same wires that brought the TV signal to them.

They could also use their televisions to do many other things, including shopping, gambling, classified advertising, playing interactive games, and home schooling. Suddenly a new marketplace was opened by digital technology: a 1993 estimate by the Yankee Group suggested that as much as $66 billion of revenues could be captured in the new interactive digital marketplace.

To position themselves to realize this revenue potential, companies in both the phone and cable industries invested tens of millions of dollars to develop the technologies that would enable them to capture the new integrated marketplace that they envisioned.

Or perhaps fantasized would be a better choice of words. After about five years of intensive development and numerous experiments with small groups of customers, interactive television is still not ready for widespread implementation.

The technology has been more difficult (and more expensive) to develop than had been expected, and it is only now nearing maturity. However, the huge costs must be amortized over a fixed customer base, and to date no business model has been found that makes sense for installing these systems on a large scale.

This realization was soon widespread, and by 1995 the bold proclamations about the compelling future of interactive television fell quiet.

But while the prospects for interactive TV were fading, the continuing evolution of computer technology and its application in digital communications has emerged in a much different way.

In effect, while crowds of people stood facing the sunrise in expectation of a great arrival from the east, a new phenomenon arrived quietly from the west, and brought with it a rupture in the world of communications. The internet came of age with the invention of the world wide web, and is in the process of becoming the new market that had once seemed to be the domain of interactive TV.

Most of the compelling qualities that were expected of interactive television are possessed by the internet, as well as some that were not envisioned. These qualities, combined with the rapid expansion of internet use has created a new mass medium that is at the same time a new kind of market.

# *Notes*

1. These ideas were presented by Dr. Russell Ackoff in his speech to the 10th annual conference of GOAL/QPC, November 8, 1993. I first presented the model in this form in *Managing the Evolving Corporation* (New York, Van Nostrand Reinhold, 1995. p. 72.) See also, Dr. Russell Ackoff, *The Democratic Corporation*. New York, Oxford University Press, 1994, and, Dr. Russell Ackoff, *Creating the Corporate Future*. New York, John Wiley & Sons, 1981.

2. Fumio Kodama, *The Techno-Paradigm Shift*. London, Pinter Publishers, 1991. Data from MITI and the Japanese Prime Minister.

3. Jim Taylor and Watts Wacker, *The 500 Year Delta*. New York, HarperBusiness, 1997.

4. Jagdish N. Sheth, and Rajendra S. Sisodia, *The Consolidation of the Information Industry – A Paradigm Shift*. Chicago, International Engineering Consortium, 1996.

5. Adapted from: Teruyasu Murakami and Takashi Nishiwaki, *Strategy for Creation*. Cambridge, England, Woodhead Publishing, 1991.

6. Noel Tichy and Stratford Sherman, *Control Your Destiny or Someone Else Will*. New York, Currency Doubleday, 1993.

7. William Manchester, *A World Lit Only by Fire: The Medieval Mind and The Renaissance*. Portrait of an Age. Boston, Little, Brown and Company, 1992, 1993.

8. Marshall McLuhan, *Understanding Media: The Extensions of Man*. Cambridge, MA, The MIT Press, 1995.

9. John Hagel III and Arthur G. Armstrong, *net gain: expanding markets through virtual communities*. Boston, Harvard Business School Press, 1997.

10. Mary Meeker and Chris Dupuy, *The Internet Report*. New York, Harper Business, 1996, and PR Newswire, February 5, 1997, and Julia Angwin, "Internet Usage Doubles in a Year." San Francisco Chronicle, March 13, 1997.

11. Mike Shatzkin, President, The IdeaLogical Company, in remarks to the 1994 Digital TV Conference, San Francisco.

12. "The Information Business" map, © 1986 Program on Information Resources Policy, Harvard University. Reprinted by permission.

13. Robert H. Frank and Philip J. Cook, *The Winner-Take-All Society*. New York, Penguin Books, 1995, p. 48.

14. Jagdish N. Sheth and Rajendra S. Sisodia, *The Consolidation of the Information Industry – A Paradigm Shift*. Chicago, International Engineering Consortium, 1996.

15. Jagdish N. Sheth and Rajendra S. Sisodia, *The Consolidation of the Information Industry – A Paradigm Shift*. Chicago, International Engineering Consortium, 1996.

16. Jon Swartz, "E-mail Outage At AOL." *San Francisco Chronicle*, June 13, 1997.

17. Retail consultant Paco Underhill as interviewed on "Fresh Air," March 26, 1997.

18. Lawrence Wilkinson, Global Business Network.

19. Blaine Harden and Anne Swardson, "Bad Dreams." *The Washington Post National Weekly Edition*, March 18-24, 1996.

20. Wired Magazine, April 1997, p. 78.

21. Dr. William L. Miller, "A Broader Mission for R&D." Research•Technology Management, November-December, 1995; and, Dr. William L. Miller and Langdon Morris, *4th Generation R&D: Managing Knowledge, Technology, and Innovation*, New York, John Wiley & Sons, 1999.

22. Philip Greenspun, *Database Backed Web Sites: The Thinking Person's Guide to Web Publishing*. Emeryville, CA, Ziff-Davis Press, 1997

23. *Technology & Media Newsletter*, Volume 1, Number 3, August, 1994.

24. Michael E. Porter, *Competitive Advantage: Creating and Sustaining Superior Performance*. New York, Free Press, 1985; and, Michael E. Porter, Competitive Strategy: Techniques for Analyzing Industries and Competitors. New York, Free Press, 1980.

25. Langdon Morris, *Managing the Evolving Corporation*. New York, Van Nostrand Reinhold, 1995.

26. Mike Mills, "A Fresh View From the Top." *The Washington Post National Weekly Edition*, May 5, 1997.

27. Brian Arthur, "Increasing Returns and the New World of Business." *Harvard Business Review*, July-August 1996.

28. John Hagel III and Arthur G. Armstrong, *net gain: expanding markets through virtual communities*. Boston, Harvard Business School Press, 1997.

29. Robert B. Reich, *The Work of Nations*. New York, Vintage Books, 1991, 1992, p. 83.

30. Julia Angwin, "Internet Usage Doubles in a Year." *San Francisco Chronicle*, March 13, 1997.

31. Jon Katz, "Birth of a Digital Nation." *Wired Magazine*, April 1997. p. 49.

32. George Gilder, *Life After Television*. New York, W.W. Norton, 1992.

33. Fumio Kodama, *Emerging Patterns of Innovation*. Boston, Harvard Business School Press, 1991, 1995.

34. Philip Greenspun, *Database Backed Web Sites: The Thinking Person's Guide to Web Publishing*. Emeryville, CA, Ziff-Davis Press, 1997.

35. Jagdish N. Sheth and Rajendra S. Sisodia, *The Consolidation of the Information Industry — A Paradigm Shift*. Chicago, International Engineering Consortium, 1996; The New York Times, April 23, 1994.

# *Index*

# About the Author

Langdon Morris is a Partner of Knowledge Venture Partners (www.knowledgeventures.com).

He is author of *Managing the Evolving Corporation* (Van Nostrand Reinhold, 1995), co-author of *4th Generation R&D: Managing Knowledge, Technology, and Innovation* (John Wiley & Sons, 1999), and a Contributing Editor of *Knowledge Management Magazine*.

Key contributions to this report were made by Hervé Utheza, Pascal R. Baudry, and William L. Miller.

www.ingramcontent.com/pod-product-compliance
Lightning Source LLC
Chambersburg PA
CBHW051100050326
40690CB00006B/763